By the Grace and command of the Guru

Mahamantra As I See It

Sriram R

Mahamantra As I See It

Author: Sriram R

Published by:

Global Organization for Divinity (G.O.D.) USA

3363 Bel Mira Way, San Jose CA 95135

Phone: (830) 4 GOD USA

Email: contact@godivinity.org

Website: www.godivinity.org

Copies also available at:

Houston Namadwaar Prayer House

3642 Bailey Ave, Manvel TX 77578

Phone: 281-402-6585

Email: houston.god@godivinity.org

ISBN-13:978-0692621363 (Global Organization for Divinity)

ISBN-10:0692621369

First edition: 2016

His Holiness Maharanyam Sri Sri Muralidhara Swamiji

This book is dedicated at the lotus feet of my beloved Master

Acknowledgements

I'm forever indebted to my Master for blessing me with this service and for inspiring and enabling me to write this book.

My deepest gratitude to Sri M K Ramanujamji for providing constant guidance and motivation, and also for the final editing of the book, despite his busy schedule and worldwide travel engagements during Fall/Winter 2015.

Huge thanks to my wife, Nisha Giri, for being my sounding board on a daily basis, and for editing the book and giving it the right finishing polish. Special thanks as well to my mother-in-law, Mrs. Nirmala Giri, for her motivation and feedback.

Heartfelt thanks also to Dr. Janani Vasudevan for the cover page design, and to her and Dr. Bhagyanathanji for the pictures.

Blessing Message from the Master

His Holiness Maharanyam Sri Sri Muralidhara Swamiji

Sri Hari:

'Mahamantra As I See It' is a very lucid account that stands testimony to the deep devotion and love that Chi. Sriram has towards the Sadguru and the Mahamantra. The transformations in his life, the personal experiences of Guru's Grace, his faith in the Mahamantra, have all been beautifully and poetically expressed in a very interesting manner. His sincerity and frankness in sharing his journey in this path of Faith is sure to inspire many more seekers as they go through this book, which is gripping till the end. The bud of love and faith that was latent in his heart and blossomed into a flower, has now found fruition as this book. May Lord Krishna shower His boundless blessings on Sriram and his family to serve Him and Mahamantra forever.

Margashirsha Swathi Day
January 2016

Contents

My Master

Ancient Indian texts describe God's head as one made out of an ingredient called Love[1]. If my Master's incarnation had descended at that time, I bet they would have said it a little differently - an entire body made of Love[2]!

From head to toe, the Master is filled with Love. Be it to the commoner, the peasant, the farmer, the road-sweeper, the movie star, a corporate bigwig, an artist or musician, a politician, the prime minister, a Vedic scholar and every unsaid soul in between, man or woman, animal or bird, his love radiates and permeates equally to everyone, everywhere. His every action, every gesture, every thought, every decision is grounded in love, for he is the personification of love, not just in the head, but in his entirety!

---

[1] *Priyameva shira:* - The Upanishads
[2] *"Priyameva sharira:"*

In my wildest dreams I could never have imagined that I would know, see, and speak to such a One, whose very association removes all hatred and fills us – the most downtrodden – with Love and Grace.

~~

The Master's qualities are innumerable, but out of his infinite grace, I dare to share a handful that have shaped my view of the Divine. I mentally prostrate to my Master, and pray to pardon any mistakes and misinterpretations I have committed.

~~

Once we had arranged for a meeting of a man with the Master in connection to a project we were doing abroad. The man had expected the "Swamiji" to have an aura around him; attendants tending to every bit of the Swamiji's needs; protocols to be followed to meet him; the Swamjii to be one dressed in an ochre robe and seated on a giant throne; sporting a long beard, long hair and expensive paraphernalia fitting a modern day textbook 'Indian saint'. Needless to say, the visitor was quite disappointed.

When he went to Premika Bhavanam[3], he couldn't believe what he saw. There was the Master seated in an ordinary chair in a corner, dressed in a simple white *dhoti*[4], wearing plain *tulasi* beads on his broad chest, and a radiant face adorned with *gopi chandana*. He had nothing to flaunt his greatness other than perhaps a warm welcome smile. The visitor didn't believe this could be a 'Swamiji', for all his conventional expectations had been shattered. The man never returned to the Master, nor has he expressed any interest afterwards. But I felt reassured with the man's description of his visit. I was then more drawn to the Master.

This episode also revealed to me that somehow or the other, when someone does some work that has pleased the Almighty, they are blessed with the association or *darshan*[5] of the Master. This gentleman from the US had constructed several temples, and was a well-known architect in the circle of the divine. Perhaps that service towards the grander purpose of *Sanatana Dharma*[6] had

---

[3] The Master's abode and place of satsang in Chennai, India
[4] Traditional Indian male clothing, usually white in color
[5] Holy sight or meeting
[6] The Vedic way of life that has been prevalent in the Indian subcontinent for thousands of years; which was later given the name of Hinduism by western researchers.

pleased the Lord, and the cosmos gave him the blessing of a darshan of the Master.

~~

Once during my early days in *satsang*[7], I went to Premika Bhavanam. The small upper-story hall was packed with devotees, say upwards of a couple of hundred. At one point, a well-dressed man walked up to the Master and offered him something. As the Master always accepts anything we offer to him with love, he accepted the man's offer and kept it aside. When the Master saw what was in it, he was instantly repulsed and disgusted. He called an attendant and dismissed the bag to him with a quick expression of distaste. It made me very curious about what it was that made the Master react this way. As I was thankfully sitting quite close, I was able to decipher that it was a bag of cash. The Master wasn't happy about receiving it. He asked for it to be returned to the man as soon as possible. There was no fuss, no drama, in this entire episode. It all happened in a matter of seconds. I didn't need

---

[7] Literally, association with the Truth. Used to indicate association with a Guru and fellow devotees

to research more on why this happened. But I felt good being there in his truly divine company.

~~

From the moment my Master's *kirtans*[8] came out in "Madhura Gitam" CDs, I instantly developed love for them. I would eagerly await the release of a new song, a new CD. I would listen to it over and over again, and read the lyrics a dozen times to quickly familiarize myself with it. I was never trained in music, and my knowledge was limited only to listening and reproducing without the nuances of the *raga* or *tala*[9]. Nevertheless, I completely enjoyed his kirtans and never missed a chance to indulge myself and others in singing them to my heart's content. The Master never knew about my interest in his kirtans. Or so I thought. Until a particular incident gave me a different perspective on what he knows and knows not.

On an autumn evening in 2011, I went to have his darshan at Premika Bhavanam. It was about 5 PM. There was barely another soul in there then. The Master was seated in his favorite corner, next to the window, looking

---

[8] Devotional songs. The term is also used to denote devotional chanting
[9] Stipulated musical patterns and rhythms in Indian music

out into the street below. I sat down leaning against the short wall perpendicular to him. I don't know why, but somehow my mind was racing hard. I felt like that could be the day that I could sing to the Master; but it was so naïve and silly for someone like me, who could never impress this great connoisseur with my plain voice, to imagine that possibility. But I kept wrestling this in my mind back and forth, and was trying to decide on a song, should the Master himself ask me to sing something.

Yes, I was insane! The odds of that happening was zero. I knew it. Yet there I was, filtering out the list of songs to narrow down to one that I should sing. After a lot of internal debate, I decided on this beautiful kirtan of the Master - "*Palli Paruvathil*". A song on Lord Srinivasa. I mentally ran through the words a couple of times to ensure I would not stammer in between. I breathed a sigh of relief when I was ready.

That very instant, the Master got up from his chair, gave me a smile and walked over to the altar. He called for a *bhagavata*[10] who was there at the time. And he asked him

---

[10] A person who sings solely for God

16

to sing that exact song that I had narrowed down - *Palli Paruvathil*! I sat there in utter disbelief!

Once that was sung, the Master went inside, and there was no other kirtan sung in satsang that day. Just that one. I was stunned, not knowing how that very song was chosen by the Master! But it reassured me that he knows everything – even unsaid words. I've heard long-time disciples say that the Master has said that he knows our thoughts even before it originates in us; needless to say then about thoughts that are prominently surfaced and wrestled through for 15 minutes in his very presence!

So compassionate that he is, he took even this simple desire that sprouted in my heart, and reflected it back in a way that assured me that he knows me in and out. The fulfillment of the desire was actually not so significant, but what stood out was the fact that he came to my level of comprehension and connected with my heart.

~~

One of the greatest qualities of the Master that is closest to my heart is his outpouring of compassion towards simple-minded folk. In 2013, during the *janavasam*[11]

---

[11] Pre-wedding ceremony

procession at the Janmashtami Brahmotsav[12] in Madhurapuri[13], the Master was relaxed and conversing with nearby bhagavatas on variety of topics, as he walked at the head of the procession. The *nadaswaram* troupe was playing auspicious wedding songs for the Divine Groom, Sri Premika Varadan[14], who was being carried majestically in a grand palanquin.

I happened to be in close proximity of the Master out of utmost fortune. It was a hot, muggy end-of-summer evening in brutal August, with a sea-crowd of thousands of devotees walking all around the Master. Unless one was completely enamored by the darshan of the Lord and the Master (which was true of all the thousands there), it was sure to be a difficult evening of sweating discomfort. The Master was chatting casually with his dearest bhagavatas and listening to the *nadaswaram*[15] tunes. A little later, I noticed a sudden change in the Master's demeanor. He became quiet, and didn't say anything for a few minutes.

---

[12] An annual 10-day festivity at the Master's Ashram that begins on Janmashtami – the day of Lord Krishna's birth.
[13] The Master's Ashram in the outskirts of Chennai
[14] Sri Premika Varadan- Sri Madhuri Sakhi are Lord Krishna and Sri Radha Devi worshipped by the Master, who have Their abode at Madhurapuri Ashram.
[15] A double-reed wind instrument commonly played at south Indian weddings

During the Master's procession rounds in the Brahmotsav, a few men from the nearby village generally perform the service of fanning the Master and the Lord. These fans are called Govinda *chamarams*[16] because they have "Govinda" inscribed on them in large lettering. There are usually about six men who do this service. They generally stand behind the Master's circle of bhagavatas and others who carry the Lord's palanquin. With these tall fans, they keep the area around the Master and the palanquin breezy. These fans, that are over 10 feet tall, are large, heavy and uncomfortable to constantly work for more than 10 minutes at a time; yet those men wield them for hours together.

That day, the six of them were constantly fanning away; sweating all over without the slightest relief of cool breeze on themselves, but all their energies fully focused on keeping the Lord comfortable. As the Master walked down the steps of the Kanyakumari Sri Jaya Hanuman temple[17] and stood there for a minute, he observed one of the village men profusely dedicated to the fanning. He saw him and

---

[16] Extended hand fans woven from banana or palm leaves
[17] A large 24-feet high Hanumanji situated next to Madhurapuri Ashram

19

fixed his compassionate eyes on him for a few seconds. Then turning towards one of the bhagavatas, he said softly, quoting a *sloka*[18] from Srimad Bhagavatam[19], "See how hard he's working! What is unattainable for one who has pleased the Lord?"[20]

Whose greatness should I cherish here? On one hand, this hard-working devotee showed me first-hand how selfless service pleases the Lord; on the other hand, what to say of the Master's great compassion of bestowing him with the highest – his attention, his love, his care, his everything? The Lord gave everything to the simple man who had no prayer, who had no interest in seeking the Lord's attention, who had nothing to desire except to keep the Lord cool while he himself was drowning in perspiration. I'm sure not one in the large gathering there, thought even for a second about these fanners; none except the One whose thought really matters. Can there be any doubt that the fanner's life had been completely filled with divine grace from that very instant? Till date, I don't think that man, who was the

---

[18] Sanskrit verse.
[19] Srimad Bhagavatam Purana is a beautiful Indian scriptural text that contains the stories of great devotees, and of Lord Krishna Himself. It shows the path of Bhagavata Dharma, which entails listening to the Lord's stories and chanting His Names.
[20] *kim alabhyam bhagavati prasannE srIniketanE – Srimad Bhagavatam (SB) 10.39.2*

recipient of this grace, knows the Master's thought and blessings on him; but we know for sure that his life attained its purpose that day.

~~

There is a lot more to say about the Master, even from my little eyes, and pray that by his mercy, we'll see more throughout this book. But one thing that begs to be told here is his purpose and his vision of the world. This too stems from his unbounded love and compassion for all life forms. We could approach this in two ways. One, by simple blind faith, or secondly by our own introspection based on our experiences.

The former is the shortcut. Yes, it is true that the Supreme has incarnated to establish *dharma*[21] in Kali Yuga[22]. If we can grasp this right away, we are blessed. This book will then give that bliss one experiences when someone they love is talked about.

---

[21] Righteousness; duty; the right path for this Age
[22] The current Age, which is the final Age in the Hindu cycle of four Ages. This, according to the scriptures, will be filled with corruption, pollution, misery and deterioration of man's mind and lifespan.

But the latter approach is how I viewed it when I came in. And from my own experience have developed belief and faith in his purpose and vision.

We affectionately call the Master 'Guruji'. This word Guruji reminds me of a song written by a devotee of the Master many years ago. She sings, "When I hear the word 'Guruji', my heart fills up with happiness."[23] How true that rings! Being a Guru is a huge part of who the Master is.

The Master says that a Guru may do many activities, but his sole purpose is to turn the vision of his disciples away from the world and towards God; that transformation is the prime work of any Guru, regardless of the means that may be applied.

But calling our Master a "Guru" alone feels insufficient if that word limits the reach of his work to the small list of disciples treading a spiritual path. The Master's purpose is not only for those select few direct disciples. It is to uplift everyone in the world. Truly a *jagad-guru* (Master to the whole world), in the entire sense of the word. The same scriptures of Sanatana Dharma that say it is rare to get a human birth, rarer to seek liberation, and rarer still to

---

[23] Original song in Tamil - *Guruji endra sollai kettaal, ullathil anandam pongudhe*

have the association of a saint, also say that there is a simple path to attain the Lord – in this difficult Kali Yuga – for all, without exception. So, while being a Guru for the seekers is for the benefit of those select few, the larger majority in the world also need a savior. Both of these are accomplished by the Master, and I might add, truly only by the Master.

Kalau Keshava kIrtanAt![24] In this day and age, chanting the Divine Names is the way to attain the purpose of life, declare the scriptures. To our Master, everything revolves around the Divine Name. He is the happiest when he is chanting, or hearing someone chant, the Names of God. The Master often says that to know the message of a book or a lecture, it is important to note how it starts, how it ends, what is in the heart of it, what is repeated often, and what has been emphasized. If we applied the same to the Master's life, we can clearly see that his journey is bookended by the Mahamantra[25], he talks most often

---

[24] *yat phalam nAsti tapasA na yogEna samAdhinA*
tat phalam labhate samyak kalau kEshava-kIrtanAt – Bhagavata Mahatmyam (BM) 1.67
The Fruit (result) that is very difficult to obtain even with great penance, yoga or meditation, that Fruit can be attained easily simply by chanting the Names of God, in this Kali Yuga.
[25] *Hare Rama Hare Rama Rama Rama Hare Hare*
Hare Krishna Hare Krishna Krishna Krishna Hare Hare
In this book, the terms Mahamantra, Nama and Divine Name are used interchangeably.

about Mahamantra, he sings about the Mahamantra, he writes about the Mahamantra, his *upadesa* (spiritual instruction) is with the Mahamantra, and his favorite people are those who chant the Mahamantra. His whole purpose is to spread this Nama (the Divine Name) to the whole world.

His love, his purpose, his vision couldn't be put any more succinctly than these words of the Master himself to a devotee. "There are two types of people in this world - the ones who are chanting the Lord's Names, and the ones who will be chanting the Lord's Names."

This is the vision of the Master - the one who came down from his abode to take all ashore through the dharma prescribed for this Age – *Nama Sankirtan* (chanting the Divine Names). And through this journey, we get to enjoy the great qualities of the Almighty - the compassion, the love, the simplicity, the humility, the humor, the beauty... the whole package.

Background

Human life is rare! The Master says this all the time with great emphasis on the word 'rare'. I vividly remember the time it hit me. When the Master was giving a discourse on Srimad Bhagavata Mahatmyam[26], he recited two Sanskrit verses that spoke of the value of a human birth.[27]

As he spoke, he got immersed in these verses and could not move past them. He spoke on this for the entire duration of the two-hour discourse with constant re-emphasis on the rarity of human life and the need to lose our affinity to the body. This talk made a huge difference in my perception.

---

[26] Bhagavata Mahatmyam (BM) is a set of chapters from the Padma Purana (a scriptural text) that speak about the greatness of another scriptural text, Srimad Bhagavata Purana.

[27] *dehEsthi mAmsarudhirEbhimatim tyaja tvam... – BM 6.79*
Cease you to identify yourself with the body consisting of bones, flesh and blood...

durlabho mAnusho deho dehinAm kshaNabhangura... – SB 11.2.29
The human body is extremely rare to achieve, and can be lost at any moment...

For the first 25 years of my life, I had lived without hearing even a mention about the presence of this *mahatma* (saint) right in the same city as I lived then - Chennai. I still lament to this day on all the missed opportunities. But then providence is never wrong. I guess the fact is, I wasn't ready until it happened in 2002. Or so I think. The reason for my uncertainty is that they say the association of a Guru in our lives is not just something that starts only in this life. His protection and care of us is through many lives, and could often remain undetected by us, until the time it needs to be revealed. The whole game is quite fascinating to consider.

Even in the days prior to me meeting the Master, on retrospection, I could relate to his divine hand being in my life. When I was in the crossroads of high-school and college, I suffered a serious bout of chicken pox, which ruined most of my critical entrance examinations to various colleges. Despite having a very good score in my 12th grade, I could not get admission into any engineering college. Then by some sure hand of God, I got admission to a college with the recommendation of a high ranked public official. The college I was admitted into was Annamalai University, the alma mater of my own Master! And even more intriguingly, the person who helped me join Annamalai University resigned her high profile job the very next day (after recommending me to this college). She resigned to take up a life of renunciation and went to Tiruvannamalai to pursue spiritual practice under the guidance of none other than Yogi Ramsuratkumar Maharaj. Yogiji, another great mahatma, had a very close bond with my Master. And even today, many years after Yogiji's passing, my Master often visits Yogiji's Ashram in Tiruvannamalai and is revered greatly by his disciples there. It doesn't take a genius to connect the dots here about the hand of the Master in this episode.

I now proudly say that I have a great connection with the Master, because we are alumni of the same college! During weekends in those 4 years of college life, I used to frequently visit my uncle and aunt in Cuddalore, as it was only an hour away from Chidambaram, where Annamalai University was located. In Cuddalore, my uncle's house was in an area called Manjakuppam, and – believe it or not – the house was within a stone's throw from the birth place of the Master; the house that he grew up in! Of course, I didn't know all this until much later, but I cite this to show that the Master has surely been watching me even before I came to Him.

~~

The Master often says that the mother is the first Guru of a child. She's the one who takes the child to the temple, shows him to the Lord, teaches him to pray, to chant slokas[28], circumambulate the temple, wear religious marks on the forehead, respect the *prasad*[29], perform *puja*[30], and so forth. My household was no different. Despite trying family conditions in a challenging joint-family life, my mother was a great source of culture and wisdom, for she always ensured that I had the grounding in our dharma which would help me in the future. I never learned to respect that, until I was a lot older and heard it straight from the Master.

The Master may not say a word directly to us, but he somehow ensures that his message touches the heart and we reflect on it for our own spiritual growth. It is common

---

[28] In this context, Sanskrit verses chanted as prayers. An inherent part of worship in the Hindu tradition.
[29] Remnants of sacred offerings to God
[30] Worship

to hear about gratitude to parents for various things – for education, for clothing, for shelter, for taking care of our health, being with us during ups and downs, etc., but it is only through the Master's talks that I learned that the first gratitude for taking us to God should be to the mother, for she sowed the seeds of bhakti in us when we were little. After all, haven't our parents been primarily responsible to get us started on the journey towards achieving the purpose of our lives?

I have to be very thankful for one more thing. When I came to the Master, I had "no spiritual baggage". I didn't have any preconceived notions or strong affiliations to any deity, saint, temple, etc. When I grew up, religion was always there in the background – but only to lead a life of faith, sufficient enough to celebrate festivals, pray during difficulties, and make periodic trips to the holy places.

This kind of an upbringing was a blessing in a way, because it ensured that I didn't have any rigid ideologies about religion. I figured there was a God, but I didn't know much else. I knew some slokas, but I didn't know His qualities; I knew the religious routines, but I didn't know their purpose; I knew some of the Lord's stories, but I didn't know the *rasa*[31]; I knew some *bhajans*[32], but I didn't know that the Lord loved it so much; I knew about some saints' lives, but I didn't get a tinge of inspiration from any of it. I did all that I did for either satisfying my family tradition, or to win prizes in competitions. That said, I was never forced to do all this, nor did I hate it. It wasn't like I rebelled. I was just never oriented towards something grander. So over the course of growing up, everything quietly faded away as 'greater' priorities in life took over.

I see this as a blessing because when I went to the Master in my late twenties, my slate was clean. Anything he wrote on it just got etched without me having to erase past misplaced spiritual notions – true or otherwise. For that, I'm deeply thankful, because I now see friends struggle to accept and adopt the Master and his simple message because of the burden of past impressions which are like mountains to get over.

I chose to share my background here to show that the love of the Master is not restricted to some 'eligible' souls only. In fact, my life was perhaps the most pedestrian

---

[31] The beauty, sweetness
[32] Devotional songs

of all and yet he chose to shower his grace for no apparent reason. We don't need any skills, wealth, social ranks, talent, beauty, qualities, or any qualifiers to uniquely separate us from the crowd to draw his attention. The Master's nature is *soulabhya* – easily accessible. His grace is there for the whole world, even to the most mundane person; for it is not about the disciple's virtues, but entirely about the Master's.

How I came to the Master

The Master says in his lectures that a Guru is not one for whom we can put an advertisement in the classified sections of the newspaper. Especially in today's times, when a lot of 'fake' institutions and swamis – who profess spiritual goals but only seek worldly pursuits – come out left, right and center, it is scary to venture out ourselves in search of a Guru. People are wary with the very mention of the word 'Guru' because so many of these so-called god-men end up being eventually exposed as frauds going after money, power, and fame.

Only the most valuable things are impersonated, the Master says. We may not see fake Timex watches, but a Rolex surely has a slight variant - Rodex! If we fail to find the real diamond for fear of the fakes, who is the real loser? Does it in any way diminish the glory of the diamond one bit? Certainly not. The fear of the fake Guru is perhaps only a means to weed off the fake seeker. The Master says that we are corrupt in every other quest, should we be that way even in the quest for God? When we *truly* seek the Lord, a true Guru will be sent.

~~

I was once driving with a senior disciple of the Master in the United States. We were talking on a variety of topics, and suddenly there was a few minutes of silence. I had been pondering the great question of "How did 'I' come to the Master?" I have no qualifications, no interest... why me? How me? I asked him this question with a genuine need to find the answer. Without blinking an eye, he replied, "Somehow you were associated with a *sadhu*[33] and that connection was all that was needed."

That devotee was none other than my mother-in-law. When the Master takes one in a family, he cares for all. Even if only one is deeply interested in his *sat-sang* (company of the Truth), the Master pours his love to all in the household. The Master once said jokingly, "I left one family and now I have gained all these families."

~~

---

[33] A true devotee of God

My mortal eyes first met those divine ones in early November 2002, a week before I tied the knot, in Chennai. My mother-in-law was the lone devotee of the Master in her family for more than a decade, even at that point. To her, "Guruji" was everything. The rest of her own family, and of course mine, were not disposed to 'Guru following'. Just to make her happy, I agreed to see the Master before the wedding.

Note the arrogance: "I agreed to see". Little did I know then that that day would herald the beginning of a new chapter; one that would eventually forever change my direction and vision.

With the Master, openly emotion-filled, miracle-laden meetings almost never happen. That is a beautiful part of being with the Master. It is always subtle, balanced, practical, simple and easy. Yet deeply impactful.

When the Master heard first about the would-be groom (me!), it seems he said, "Not bad, she has chosen a Vaishnava." Every word uttered by the Master is never in vain. When 'he' does the matchmaking, where is the question of our choosing? This is how the Lord works, I presume. He stays behind and gives credit to others while actually doing all the legwork in maintaining his big family.

Other than the fact that I did have darshan, I barely remember the first meeting with the Master; for as I said before, it's never dramatic. The Master blessed our wedding and out of pure compassion even attended our wedding reception despite heavy thunderstorms in the thick of the monsoon season on November 10, 2002. My wife and I, who are now ardent devotees of the Master, till date feel terrible about how inadequately we conducted ourselves when the Guru, the Lord, came for our wedding. How blessed and fortunate we were. (And how ignorant!)

When the Master came that day, there were barely two others in the large gathering who knew the Master. One was my mother-in-law, and the other one was his personal secretary who drove him there. When such was the situation, what could that poor lady do to appropriately honor the saint?

Why should the Master do these things? In Srimad Bhagavatam, the Lord says, "I am bound by My devotees!"[34] Though free, He ties himself to His devotees,

---

[34] *aham bhakta parAdhInah* – SB 9.4.63 (Ambarisha charitra)

and follows them around, bound by the chord of their love. In my case, the love of my mother-in-law. He didn't care if there wasn't any fanfare, if there wasn't any respect from anyone. He just came because this was his children's wedding.

After that initial contact, off we went, disappeared away from the clutches of anything spiritual, to that far-off land of opportunities on the other side of the world. For over four years, life was in bliss – the worldly kind, that is. It's not as if the 25 wasted years without his darshan was bad enough, I had to drain another five cruel years without any further concrete connection to the Master, despite his occasional compassionate inquiries about us through his one lone devotee in the family. The Master had blessed us to have a child and had given fruit prasad to my wife. Such was my interest in this that I don't even remember when this happened. But at one point in 2006, on his own accord, he inquired of my mother-in-law if we had had a child. Soon after, we were expecting a baby! Such is the unbounded and unconditional grace and compassion of the Master.

~~

2007 rolled around, and from then on, there was no looking back. It was the turning point for us.

In many ways, 2006-2007 timeframe, was the critical time not just for me, but many other satsang brethren and for the organization itself. I'm sure this time period in the history of the Master's *charitra* (life history) may become tabbed as the pivotal time that took his mission and movement to a larger scale. It was indeed his grace to make us a part of this as well.

This was the time that 'Namadwaar'[35] was conceptualized and many centers were established for the chanting of the Divine Names; it was the time Global Organization for Divinity was established; it was the time the Master's significant work, *Kali Dharma Undiyaar*[36], was born; it was the time the Master's Divine Padukas[37] were first blessed for the United States; it was the time when January 1 New Year Mass Prayers[38] started; it was the time

---

[35] Sanskrit for "Divine Name Entryway" – signifying a portal/entryway that leads to God through His Divine Name. Centers established by the Master around the world, for chanting the Divine Names, are called Namadwaars.

[36] A strong philosophical work that establishes logically and rationally, that the dharma/path for this Age is Nama sankirtan or chanting the Divine Names.

[37] Holy sandals of a saint or deity, that are representative of the saint or deity themselves, in this case, the Master.

[38] An inspiring discourse and prayer by the Master conducted every year on Jan 1st in a different city each year, where he extols the Mahamantra/Divine Name and urges everyone to chant it for the fulfilment of all prayers – worldly and spiritual. His talk is

when the Master's disciples began touring internationally and spreading the Master's cause everywhere, in India and abroad; it was the time that paved the way for thousands of new disciples to join the cause and be the recipients of the Master's grace.

On February 3, 2007, the devotee whose association led me to the Master, came to the USA to help with the delivery of her grandchild. On February 21, our daughter was born and since then, the Master took over. The transformation wasn't overnight by any stretch of the imagination, but it was rapid.

Everything about the Master is *madhuram* (sweet). Dr. Bhagyanathanji, the Master's personal secretary, in his *'Madhurasmaranam - My Guru as I see Him'* talks[39] says that perhaps Sri Vallabhacharya has written the *Madhurashtakam* with only our Guruji in mind; for all the verses perfectly fit the description of the Master – the looks, the gait, the words, the voice, everything about the Master is so *madhuram*. The Master's ashram is

---

usually preceded by devotees from around the world sharing their personal experiences with the Mahamantra.

[39] A series of talks Dr. Bhagyanathanji has given (and continues to give) in various places, about the Master's life.

Madhurapuri, the *tirtham*[40] is Madhurateertham, the hillock is Madhurachalam. His story is Madhura Smaranam. His kirtans are Madhura Gitam. The word Madhuramurali has several notable significances – his monthly magazine, his abode in Alapakkam (Chennai), his portal into the worldwide web, and most interesting of all is that Sri Ammalu Ammal, the (late) great contemporary saint and devotee (Kanchi Mahaperiyava[41] has hinted that she was an incarnation of Sri Purandaradasa himself), always affectionately called our Master 'MadhuraMurali'. The tag Madhuram is all his because everything about him is sweet.

When my wife and I were expecting our child, we debated a lot on the name we wanted for our yet-unborn daughter. We narrowed it down and agreed on 'Madhura'. It was our choosing! Yes, the arrogance again! At that point, we were not devotees of the Master, or into anything even remotely spiritual or satsang-related. We just lived our merry lives with no apparent purpose. We debated a lot but finally settled mutually on this 'sweet' name.

---

[40] Holy pond, lake or river usually near a temple. In this case, the pond near the Ashram.
[41] Sri Chandrashekharendra Saraswati Mahaswamiji, the famous saint and 68th pontiff of Kanchi Kamakoti Mutt

Usually, it is customary for anyone in our satsang to ask the Master for a name for their child. But for us, we didn't even consider that, to be honest. But somehow the name was chosen.

The name Brindavan is beautiful because it is associated with Krishna. Radha, Yamuna, Gokula, they are all beautiful because they have a Krishna connection. People name their houses with names related to Krishna because it is simply beautiful. They may not even be Krishna devotees, but somehow they like the name Brindavan and so they keep it. Well, there is even a train in India named the Brindavan Express (which doesn't even go to Brindavan); yet we'll be hard-pressed to find another transport so beautifully named. It was like this that we named our daughter Madhura. It just sounded beautiful. Little did we know that it derived all the beauty because of the association with MadhuraMurali!

In the Master's satsang in India, there is a lady devotee by the name of Mrs. Madhura. She is a long-time disciple of the Master. The old-timers would sometimes long for the 'golden' days when the satsangs were less crowded, and the Master was more accessible and would spend more time with them. They would sigh, "In the good old days, how Guruji used to inquire about me, talk to me, care for me, but nowadays, getting even a smile out of him is like the flowering of the *athi-poo*[42]." Mrs. Madhura was in one such mood in February 2007. It got to a point where she was literally crying that the Master didn't even remember her anymore and was dying to get some attention from him. Right at that moment, another devotee of the Master called her and exclaimed, "Do you know what Guruji has named Nirmala's granddaughter? Madhura!"

Mrs. Madhura's joy knew no bounds! She got her life back with that news. She felt so strongly that it was her Guruji who had played this *leela* (divine sport), to notify her of this at the most appropriate time! Her Guru had not forgotten her. Not only that, the lineage of the name now continued with another Madhura in the satsang!

And here we were in the US, thinking that it was we who had named this child as Madhura. The name itself was patented to the Master. What else could it be but his choosing?

~~

---

[42] Fig flower that is said to flower about once in 3000 years.

As our daughter's *namakaranam* (naming ceremony) day drew near, my mother-in-law suggested that we should perform the ceremony with only Nama, as the Master advocates, instead of the more elaborate rites that are commonly performed by Hindus. After some thought, we agreed – mainly because we were not too religious anyway, and this was rather more convenient than go all the way to a temple 50 miles away to perform some rituals we barely understood. So on the 11th day after her birth, Madhura was anointed, with all of us chanting the Mahamantra.

This was the time when the Namadwaar website -- www.namadwaar.org – had just come into existence and was being managed by a devotee in the USA. So my mother-in-law promptly sent him a picture of the 'Naming Ceremony with Nama' as a news item for the website. And interestingly, that devotee, while posting the 'news item' mentioned in it that we (my wife and I) were devoted to the Master! Well, in all honesty, that could not have been farther from the truth at that point. But now, on retrospection, it was only a forerunner of things to come.

Since our daughter was born on February 21, my mother-in-law slowly suggested to us that perhaps we could chant the Mahamantra for one hour on the 21st of every month. I'm sure it was some sneaky way to get us to chant Nama. But being new parents and all excited about our daughter's new life, we didn't think this was too bad an idea. What were we going to lose by a little chanting once a month? Still, when it was the 21st every month, the one hour would feel like one long year. Chanting 60 whole minutes of the Mahamantra was no picnic. We did it however, quite begrudgingly and mechanically. It was for people like me that the Master says that not a single Nama we chant will ever go waste. And it doesn't matter how it is delivered.

Whether we say the Names of the Lord indirectly, jokingly, as a musical entertainment, or even neglectfully, it will still immediately relieve one from the reactions of unlimited sins.[43]

The Mahamantra started to do its job on us.

~~

---

[43] *sANketyaM pArihAsyaM vA stobhaM helanameva vA*
vaikuNTha-nAma-grahaNam-asheShAghaharaM viduH – SB 6.2.14

In the summer of 2007, the Master inspired a few of his disciples to travel to the US to spread his mission. Sri Ramanujamji and Sri Poornimaji had planned their visit to the USA for the first time in Fall-Winter 2007. There were literally less than 10 devotees of the Master all around the US then. The only ones in the entire state of Texas then were my mother-in-law and another devotee in Dallas. And my mother-in-law was scheduled to return to India in August, before the messengers of the Master arrived in the US.

Before my mother-in-law left, she had meticulously arranged for 10 different programs for the Master's apostles across several different temples in Houston, including a Srimad Bhagavata Saptaham[44]! Is such a thing really possible by a visiting mother in a completely foreign land? Just this fact alone is standing proof of the Master's hand in everything that happens. His emissaries carry the Master's *tapas* (penance). All they have to do is make a small effort and the results show through in shining glory

---

[44] A traditional exposition of the Srimad Bhagavatam text that is traditionally done over 7 days

through the immense power of the Master's divine will playing through these sadhus.

And so it was that by the Master's will, these two disciples came to stay with us in Houston for a few weeks.

During that period, one fine day, I was faced with a 'moment of truth' test. I was the captain of the 'world famous' cricket team Lagaan XI of Houston's taped-ball cricket league. We had taken Northwest Houston by storm in the prior 2 seasons and were rocking away in the league cruising through to the playoffs in the Fall 2007 season.

The semifinal match was on a Saturday morning in October against the dreaded Triggers Cricket Club.

Until the previous evening, it didn't dawn on me that I had a decision to make: either drive around Sri Ramanujamji (Ramuji) for his scheduled discourses, or play my cricket match. And it was not merely playing or attendance. I was the captain! I couldn't just call someone and tell them I couldn't come! Moreover, I really wanted to play. So it was not just a question of availability. Back in the day, this was a classic *dharma-sankatam* (being torn between two 'righteous' paths/choices) for me. I called my friend and told him that I was 'tentative' for the match the next day and arranged for a stand-in, but still I secretly hoped that I would be able to play.

In the morning however, I had no questions. By divine grace and with the pleasing conversations with Sri Ramuji, it didn't even occur to me to not drive him. There was no choice. I ditched my cricket match and happily went to satsang.

Over the next two weeks, it was one joyful ride after another across all the newly-discovered temples in Houston that I had never set foot in earlier; but now visited them all with two sadhus to serve them and listen to their beautiful expositions of our dharma. We even went to a Srimad Bhagavata Saptaham every day for seven days in a temple located 50 miles away, with an 8-month-old baby in tow! It never felt burdensome. In fact, not going would have been cruel.

Back home, I was happily talking to Sri Ramuji about all my serious passions – baseball, football, Seinfeld, AR Rahman, Lord of the Rings, and what not. We talked about everything worldly at home (thanks to me), and everything spiritual when away (thanks to him). And slowly but surely I took to Ramuji.

During this time, we made a request to these two sadhus who had graced our home by divine will, to perform *annaprashanam*[45] and *akshara-abhyasam*[46] of our daughter, Madhura. They were both elated by the request and gladly performed the small ceremony at our home. Sri Ramuji fed Madhura her first solid food, and Sri Poornimaji grasped her tiny hands and wrote the Lord's Name, 'Sri Hari', initiating her into all things divine.

At that point, neither my wife nor I realized how fortunate we were. Perhaps we may never fully comprehend and appreciate the workings of the Master. From the moment our daughter was born, the Master had been sending sadhus to visit our house on a regular basis – to name her, to bathe her, to feed her, to teach her to read/write and so on. In fact, on her very first birthday, the Master himself in the form of his Divine Padukas came to bless her through yet another of his apostles, Sri Narayananji from Boston. And by the time her second birthday rolled around, the Master himself came and settled down here with us, as his Divine Padukas blessed

---

[45] Hindu rite that marks a baby's first intake of rice/solid food
[46] Hindu rite that marks a child's first introduction to the alphabet/education

personally for us. The journey continues even now, though at times we forget to reflect on the love and care he quietly continues to shower, while himself staying in the shadows.

~~

Once, Sri Ramuji happened to come across the great movie collection we had at home. He looked at each one of them and exchanged some jokes and chit-chat. Looking at all my comedy movie collections, he asked, "Do you watch all these also?" I said yes, in an apologetic tone, and we moved on.

Later when I had a chance to listen to Dr. Bhagyanathanji's recollection of the Master's visit to his house[47], he cited a similar incident where the Master asked him the same question years ago when leafing through his large western music collection. Soon enough, Sri Bhagyaji had lost his deep passion for western music.

I don't know what magic was done here in Houston that day, but that was the last year I watched regular TV, or movies or played any cricket. And all without any regret whatsoever. When I was driving Sri Ramuji the next year, he explained how this change happened. He said, "When we

---

[47] In his Madhurasmaranam CD

are deeply passionate by nature, it's a great thing because the passionate nature remains but the object of passion just changes due to the association with the divine."

Later that November, I went to India and that's when I had the real first darshan of the Master.

The Master led his devotee (sadhu) to our door; the devotee led us to the Nama; the Nama led us to sadhu *seva* (service); the seva led us back to the Master. And like a goat caught in the grasp of a tiger, our lives had no escape. But then, we were happy goats.

Faith over time

To see the Lord, one must possess either unflinching faith, or speak the truth always, or live in steadfast righteousness (dharma). Without having at least one of these three, the Lord cannot be attained, say the scriptures and saints.

Of the three, I feel the latter two are next to impossible, especially in this day and age. That leaves me with 'unflinching faith' as the only way.

However, having such faith in God, like Prahlada[48] did, is not possible for me. When I'm a slave to my senses, and associate myself only with this body, how am I going to pass the tests that Prahlada did? I need divinity to be tangible. I need it to be measurable by my senses. I need it to talk to me. I need it to relieve me of problems. I need it

---

[48] The little prince who was a great devotee and who had unshakeable faith in the Lord and His Name, despite being the son of a demon king and living in hostile circumstances not conducive to devotion.

to prove the concepts to me, by coming down to my level of comprehension, for I'm no *garbha-shriman*[49] like Prahlada.

Such a divinity is the Master, and hence I now have hope.

~~

When I met the Master in November 2007, it was different. It was not like 2002. For the first time, I somewhat craved to see him. There were pressures from the family, which led to a lot of discussions, but I took efforts to stand ground. I felt good, because I knew I was right. And when we are on the side of 'right', there is a superhuman element of strength that comes to us from the cosmos to ensure that we remain unmoved. In the first five years after our wedding, I did go to have courtesy darshans of the Master once or twice during our India visits – usually once right after we landed, and once towards the end of the vacation. But this time, for a change, I myself wanted to go... not just to mark attendance, but to be there.

The Master says in his discourses that listening about God itself may not develop devotion quickly, but

---

[49] Self-Realized at birth/while in the womb. Like Prahlada and Sage Shuka.

listening to the stories of His devotees will definitely inspire more. A small twist here is what changed my perception of this. I had listened to so many saints' stories as a child. After all, who in India has not read spiritual comic books? But that did not invoke any deep bhakti. It just entertained and put me to sleep. Then once when the Master compassionately gave a video message for a Bhagavata Saptaham we did in Houston, he said in that that it really mattered *who* was telling those stories. "If the speaker has pure bhakti, only then will the listener actually experience the story as if a movie was being screened. (And hence they will connect with the story.)" Otherwise the story won't stick.

Mahans (saints) and their appointed emissaries need to be the story tellers.

My first experience of listening to such a story was when Sri Ramuji was supposed to speak on the topic of Ramayana at Lakshmi Narayan Mandir in Houston. For the first hour though, I didn't even hear the word Rama. At that point, a few of us who went with Ramuji looked at each other and wondered if the topic was misunderstood by him. Because there needs to be at least some dotted-line link of the prelude to the main topic. But then Ramuji was talking at length about science in our scriptures as if addressing curious youngsters. Later of course, he miraculously connected it to Ramayana, which only the disciples of the Master can pull off seamlessly. That lecture however opened my 'intellectual' eyes on the roots of Sanatana Dharma.

When a new baby is born, it needs to be given some immunization shots, doesn't it? The Master says that we are reborn when we come to the Guru. It's a new life; so new shots are needed. This lecture by Ramuji was my first dose of faith injections. It was so powerful, yet painless. Till date, I lean on that scientific grounding of Sanatana Dharma.

My next doctor was Sri Poornimaji. In her own unique way of discoursing, *direct-dilse* (straight from the heart); there's no mincing words and sugar coating in her pills. The first time I teared up in a discourse was listening to her lecture on Dhruva Charitram at Houston's Meenakshi Temple. I didn't know I had that side in me. She opened up the heart and poured the tonic of Guru Mahima (Greatness of the Guru) straight into it. It hurt so bad I had to cry. So did all others in the audience. Dose 2 done.

The big doctor was the final installment in the sequence of shots. Sri Guruji. I was fortunate to be in Chennai when the Master was discoursing on Ramayana, verse by verse. It was the *Sita-apaharanam*[50] episode that day.

There are many ways to tell a story. One is the mundane story telling like I read to my daughter at bed time. Second is the story telling in *shuddha bhavam*[51] where the pure-at-heart narrate the incident in third person, like the disciples of the Master. The third kind is for Rama himself to come down to us and narrate the incident. His own story told through His own words. How would that be? Well, the Master's discourse was not even that. Here I didn't see a story being 'told'. I actually saw Rama struggling after losing Sita. It was not in my head, but out there on display. We could actually see how Rama felt when he lost Sita. That's the difference in the Master's lectures versus all others. Strike three!

~~

---

[50] Episode where the demon king Ravana kidnaps Lord Rama's wife Sita Devi while Rama and Lakshmana have been lured away.
[51] Pure feeling

Nurturing this baby along was an essential part of the growth. No one mothers us better than the Master, for his constant pouring of love and reinforcement of who he really is, solidified the bases.

Once I was out on town in Chennai with Ramuji. The Master's *soulabhya*[52] rubs off on his disciples too, I'm sure. We had just spent some casual time together in the T.Nagar area. We signed for an autorickshaw and started our journey from T.Nagar to Ramuji's apartment, which was right behind Premika Bhavanam in Jaffarkhanpet. The route back was via another famous place in Chennai – Kannamapettai, a burial ground. As the auto passed this cremation ground, Ramuji suddenly started talking to me about *tantrika*, an occult way of worship. I felt that it was a strange conversation because that's far from what happens in our satsang at all. I just listened quietly. We reached his apartment and then learned that the Master would give darshan that evening. It was around four in the afternoon. We freshened up and were ready to go to Premika Bhavanam. I asked Ramuji a question that was bothering me a lot. If two people have conflicting prayers, how would

---

[52] Easy, compassionate accessibility

God satisfy both? Ramuji looked at me and with a grin said that both would be fulfilled as long as the prayers are sincere. Just as I wondered how, he gave an example: Let's say a farmer goes to the temple and prays sincerely that it must rain, as his harvest would be in jeopardy without the rain. His whole family depended on it. At the same time, a potter walks up to the temple and prays to the Lord that it should be a bright and sunny day as his pots needed to dry out. The Lord will focus on the intent of the prayer and answer them both! It might rain to answer the farmer's prayer directly, and at the same time the potter's poverty could be resolved by some windfall fortune, or some old friend walking up to him and giving him the money that he needed. Hence both prayers would be answered, directly or indirectly. By then, it was time to go to Premika Bhavanam.

We had the divine darshan of the Master that evening, did our prostrations and I somehow found myself in the front of the hall, while Ramuji sat way in the back. Soon, one of the attendants of the Master, brought in the mic and *vyasa peetam*[53] to the front of the hall and the

---

[53] A little wooden table or stand used to place a scripture or sacred book, either while reciting from the text or while giving a discourse on the subject,

entire audience let out a collective mental hurrah that was perceptible by all! It meant guaranteed darshan for two hours and sweet discourse by the Master! (But these kinds of things have also backfired sometimes, when we learn later that the stage will be occupied by someone else, other than the Master.) We were cautiously optimistic, for nothing is guaranteed with him until it really happens!

The Master walked out of his room, and stood at the entrance to the hall with crossed feet, and gave his classic darshan while half-hugging the lucky wall, as Vishnu Sahasranama[54] chanting was going on. The ambience was indeed serene. A few minutes later, the Master sat down for the discourse and by then the hall was overflowing.

Everyone receives a message during the lectures of the Master, but the Master in his own unique way cautions the devotees to not read much into signs. Being emotional and reading too much into coincidences are a sign of mental weakness, the Master says. But the Hindu culture relies heavily on these things – things like a flower falling from the picture of God or a temple bell ringing and many more such signs that are commonplace in the culture. I never paid

---

[54] Slokas that enumerate 1008 names of Lord Vishnu

much attention to these things. But the Master walks a fine line here. In a light vein, he says, let us see the flower go up from the floor to the top of the picture - now that would really be a divine clue or blessing! But on the other hand, the Master also acknowledges some signs as god-sent. So it does go both ways. Anything the Master says is divine, so, from that perspective, there is no superstition.

As the Master started to give his discourse, my first bout of excitement happened when, out of the blue, the Master mentioned, "Those who practice *tantrikam* go to the cremation ground and do their penance there." This was unbelievable to me! What sign was this supposed to mean? I had not heard the Master talk about such topics previously. It was unrelated to what he was talking about that day in the lecture. I felt the same strange feeling as in the auto just three hours before! Why was he talking about the exact thing that Ramuji mentioned? I turned back to look at Ramuji in complete disbelief. He smiled back.

Minutes later in the same discourse, the Master brought up a situation that God is often faced with: how to answer conflicting prayers at the same time! I turned back towards Ramuji a second time in 5 minutes, this time grinning ear to ear, because this was no longer a mere coincidence. The Master used an example in Ramayana to highlight a problem that the Lord faced and how He handled that. When Lord Sri Rama was sent away to the forest, He left happily to uphold the word of His father. At the same time, His brother Bharata placed a sincere prayer to Rama to come back and rule the kingdom. How could Rama grant both these at the same time? In such a situation, the Lord did something that is equivalent to answering the intent of the prayer. He gave away his Divine Padukas as a representation of Himself to Bharata. These Padukas ended up ruling the kingdom for the 14 years that Lord Rama was away. So thus He fulfilled both His father's word and His brother's prayer.

I felt elated then for two reasons. For the double clarity that I now had on how He would answer conflicting prayers, and more importantly, I realized how the Master and his disciple have *eka-hrudayam* (one heart).

During the lecture, the Master had noticed the silent visual communications between Ramuji and myself, and curiously asked about it afterwards. "What were you two talking about with your eyes during the discourse?" We just smiled and knew that he knew what we knew.

~~

In 2008, I had the fortune of accompanying a close devotee family from Houston when they had their first darshan of the Master in Chennai. It was in the inside room in Premika Bhavanam, in late December. When all of us sat down, the Master inquired about all of them individually. After that, his first comment was, "Faith is the most important thing." This got tattooed in my mind ever since.

The Master says that if we did not have faith, even if the Lord Himself came and stood in front of us in all His four-armed glory, we would still not believe that it was really Him. Worse still, we might get scared and run away. Or assume that somebody was playing a trick on us. But on the other hand, he says, a person who has faith can see God even in a piece of stone!

Faith is the key in seeing and appreciating the Lord. It's the same about seeing the Master too.

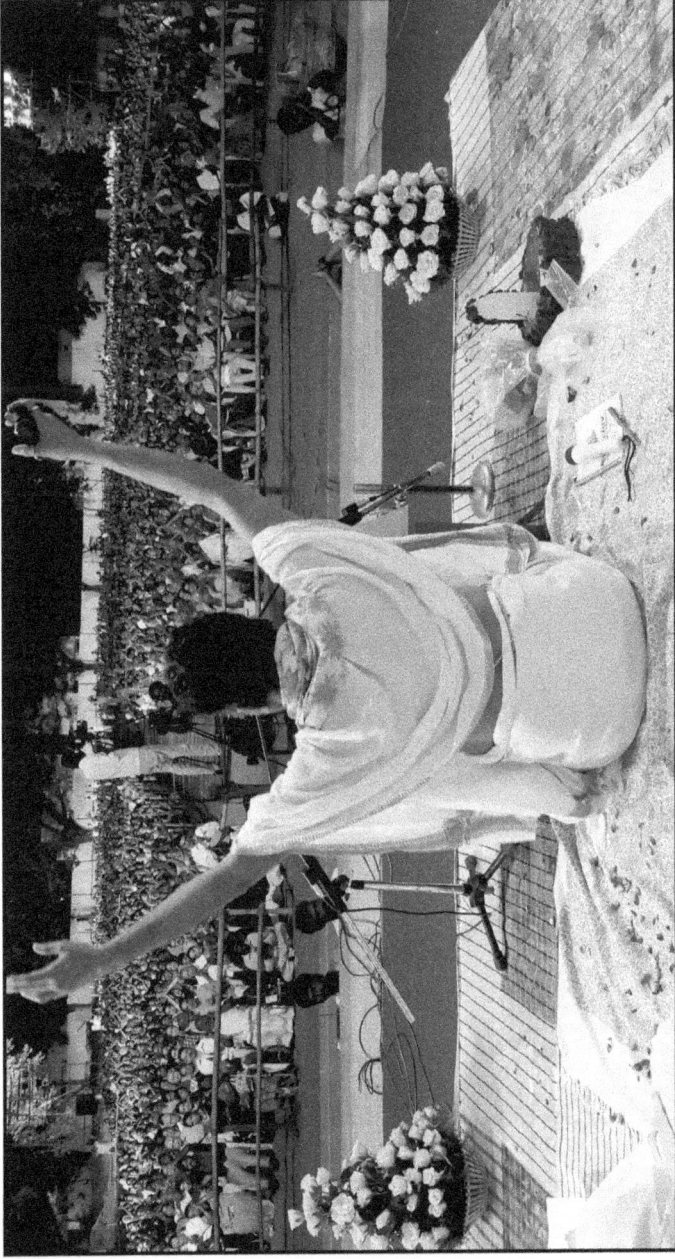

Thousands chanting the Mahamantra with the Master during a Mass Prayer at Madurai, India. January 1, 2016

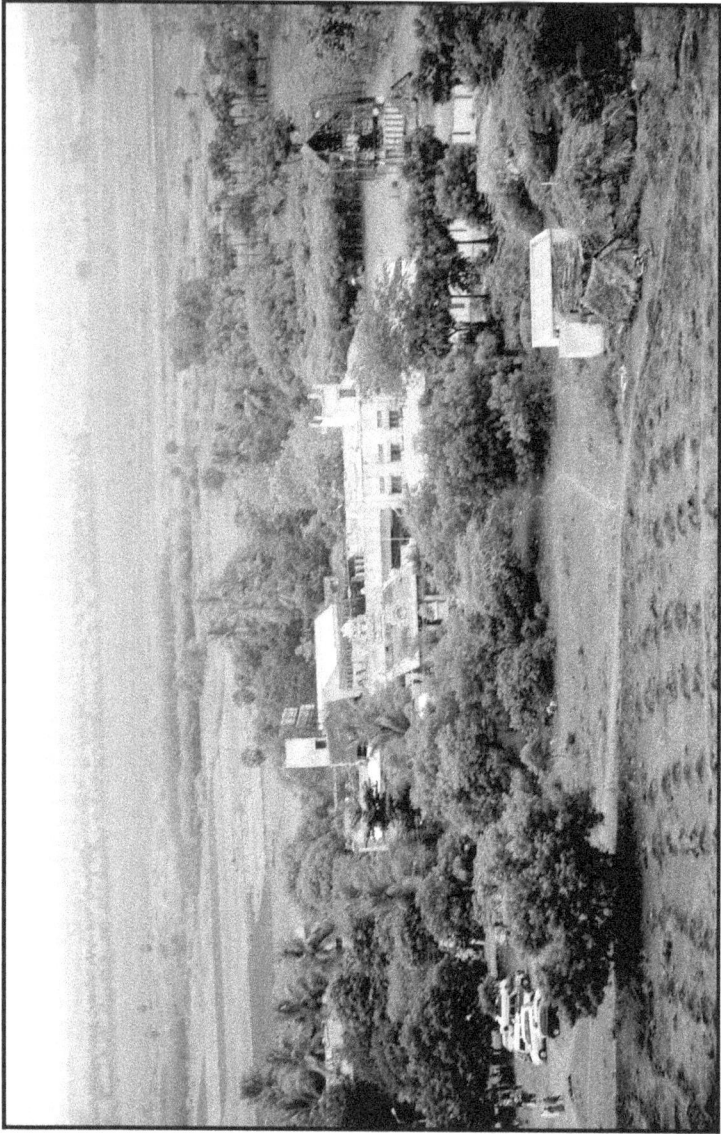

Aerial view of Madhurapuri Ashram located just outside Chennai, India

Bhagavata Bhavanam, the court of
Sri Premika Varadan-Sri Madhuri Sakhi, at Madhurapuri Ashram.

The Master seated on the *pyol* of Madhuvanam, his
living quarters at the Ashram.

Roadside view of Houston Namadwaar in 2013.
Inset: Sri Premika Varadan-Sri Madhuri Sakhi who arrived in Houston in 2015

February 14, 2010. "Nama Pravesha" ("Entry of the Divine Name") opening ceremony of Houston Namadwaar—the first Namadwaar that was established outside of India.

"16 words the Mahamantra Nama
16 people came to Nama pravesha
16 kalas of Lord Krishna evident, when
16 nazhika past midnight did Sri Swamiji see this all!"

An ode to this significant event by Sri M K Ramanujamji (pictured above standing next to Sri Swamiji's photograph).

'Elevate the Perspective'

The Master often refers to a sloka from Bhagavata Mahatmyam[55] in his talks and says - the magical gem called *'chintamani'* can bestow any worldly thing one wishes for, but nothing more. The heavenly tree called *'kalpataru'* can even bestow anything heavenly, but nothing more. But no one knows where these two are. However, even greater than these so-called wish-yielding objects is the Guru, who is visible in front of us! If he is somehow pleased with us, that can bestow on us even the highest abode – *'Vaikunta'* (Permanent Happiness).

The Master says that pleasing a guru is not about impressing him with a skill, or an art, or doing some action,

---

[55] *chintAmaNir loka sukham suradruhu swarga sampadam*
prayacchati guruhu prIto vaikunTam yOgi durlabham – BM 1.8

etc. After all, it shouldn't be surprising that the creator of the world should be happy about everything we do in the world. Which artist wouldn't enjoy their work being appreciated or put to use?

Let alone the fact that the Master is the greatest *rasika* (connoisseur) mankind has seen; pleasing the Guru here has a different meaning. The Master cites the example of yet another great saint, Sri Ramana Maharshi, and how a dog called Jackie, a cow Lakshmi, a deer Valli, crows, monkeys, and tigers were all recipients of his grace. There are even *samadhis*[56] for some of these animals in Ramanashramam[57]! What could have they done to receive their Master's grace and attain the abode of the Lord? There is no answer to this, because the Guru's grace needs no reason.

The Master is pleased by many things. Among those, a few things connect very closely to me as well. One is *'Ekanta Bhakti'* (one-pointed devotion). "Accept all, Adopt one," the Master says. The idea of adopting one starts with the acceptance of all. The Master does this so perfectly.

---

[56] sacred tombs constructed for God-Realized souls
[57] Sri Ramana Maharshi's ashram at Tiruvannamalai, Tamil Nadu

Once I had the fortune of walking with the Master. He was inquiring about a few things and suddenly said, "You see these trees? One is a mango tree, the other there is a neem tree, and there is a coconut tree. There is so much variety in trees. But when you go up to the sky and have an aerial view, how do they look? You don't see neem or mango. They are all green. When we elevate our perspective, there are no differences. Elevate our perspective." In his own unique way of conversation, the Master ended with a question, "Tell me, what did I say?" I repeated, "Elevate our perspective."

I always thanked the stars for lack of 'baggage' when I came to the Master. This helped me align very quickly to the one-pointedness. Whenever the Master speaks in his lectures about the greatness of such devotion, it tugs very closely to me.

But just as I thought that one-pointed devotion means that our love for God should be towards one particular deity, the Master takes it up a notch. He says, "Mira Bai did not even worship another form of Krishna other than Giridhari. This is Ekanta Bhakti!" It's not that Mira Bai, or our Master for that matter, are narrow in their perspectives. They know quite well that it is all the same 'green' - be it Giridhari, or Rasa Vihari, or Damodara, etc. It is the acceptance of all as One that leads them to show their love to one; and showing their love to one is needed in bhakti.

The Master says that if one wishes to find water, it is fruitless to drill 10 feet in a hundred different places. It is prudent to drill in one location, and go down hundreds of feet. We are sure to find water there. Likewise, to connect with divinity, the Master advises to catch hold of one, and only one path.

He shows the simple path of *Bhagavata Dharma*[58]. The highlight in the Master's perspective that drives the point home about equality is that, a true seeker in this path will be steadfast in his quest, but will never once say anything negative about other paths. This is the greatness of Bhagavata Dharma. Truly Accept All, and Adopt One.

~~

How can one identify a true *jnani*[59] or mahatma? The Master quotes Sri Ramana Maharshi's *Ulladhu*

---

[58] The path of bhakti through chanting the Divine Names) and listening to the Lord's stories.
[59] One who has attained *jnana* or Self-Knowledge

Naarpadhu poem where he says *'There are no identifying characteristics or marks for a jivan mukta*[60].*'* The Master adds, "Even if Bhagavan himself has said in the Gita and Bhagavatam about the characteristics of a jnani, still, there is nothing definite about the mold in which they should fit."

Sometimes they remain quiet, sometimes they sing and dance in ecstasy, at times they are serious and at other times playful, on some occasions they are very easy to approach, and some other times fearful to talk to or even go near; they could wear tatters and lie in a corner of the road amidst sewage, or they could be seated in a royal throne in the most expensive clothing; they could be 5 years old or 105 years old; man or a woman. In short, there is nothing external that identifies them.

They don't have a need to have an ashram, or devotees, or attendants, but they could also have all of these in abundance. They neither need to go on pilgrimages, nor can we expect them to be stationed in a 'holy' place at all times. They could be in perennial meditation, or not.

---

[60] Literally, one who has attained Liberation while still alive; in other words, a *jnani*

So how can we identify the great ones? Thankfully the Master gives us a few clues here. One, the Master says, look at their life history. While we can't figure by looking for things about them, we can see their history. The Master quotes the impeccable lives of devotees like Mira Bai and Bhadrachalam Ramadas who actually underwent untold suffering and even went to prison, but still when we look back at their lives, in or out of imprisonment, their devotion to the Lord stayed constant... or only became stronger!

Secondly, the adherence to scriptures. Their words and actions will resonate perfectly with the scriptures. The Master says that a mahan's words will always have some *pramana* (reference to and validation in the scriptures), so much so that the scriptures themselves use mahans' words as validity or proof of authenticity. The Master often quotes Sri Ramana Maharshi again here, who left home at the age of 16, and did not learn Sanskrit or any scripture. Yet when he realized the Supreme State, all his works naturally had testimony in the scriptures. This is the sign of a true mahatma.

The Master says, "Can the fact that one can predict the future make one a jnani? Or because they can read our minds? Are they jnanis because they can do miracles?" The Master answers his own question, "The fact that one does miracles should automatically mean they are *ajnanis* (unrealized)." The Master continues, "Is it greater for the mahan to do the miracle and get fame and glory, or completely have the capability to do miracles and yet not show it at all?" The latter is how a true mahan works. They are not swayed by name, or fame, or self-interest, but the only thing that would move them is God. Sadly, the way the world moves nowadays is that fancy miracles have become the passing grade for sainthood.

In the Master's company, we don't witness miracles, we witness compassion; we don't see predictions, we experience grace. What I mean is that even when we do experience a miraculous turn of events, it doesn't register as something extra-ordinary that the Master has done, even though he may have very well done that. Only the compassion and unconditional love registers.

~~

The Guru's grace takes two forms. One as a substratum that is foundationally conducting our lives.

Swirling in *Maya*[61], we forget this truth. The second form is the palpable one – the one that we experience during prayers. Truly, there is no difference between the two forms of grace but there appears to be a difference because of our limited capability to perceive it all the time. The Master quotes the story of a few devotees who went to have the darshan of Sri Ramana Maharshi. When they were in the saint's presence, a monkey came out of nowhere and took away a devotee's bag, resulting in a mad chase and scramble to recover their belongings. The ordeal lasted a few hours and their peace was totally lost in this quest. It was almost the end of the day and having lost hope they came back and sat in the satsang with earnest prayers in their hearts.

Sri Ramana Maharshi was always loving to the animals in the ashram, and they obeyed him too. All it took was a call from the saint and the monkey promptly came over to the hall and returned the bag. The devotees fell profusely at the feet of the Maharshi with tears in their eyes.

---

[61] The Lord's mysterious deluding power

The Maharshi later explained that the ways of God are unique. Unless people experience sorrow, grace is not palpable to them. It's not that the grace was newly discovered. It was always there, but for the devotees to realize it, such an act (of sorrow and rescue) was necessary. Without this incident, the devotees would never have connected to the saint's grace, even though it was ever present.

Even sorrow is a blessing, for without it, they would have sat there for a few minutes or hours, and left. They would have received the grace, no doubt, but this experience ensured they felt it. That tangible connection builds strength, and faith.

Once I was deeply depressed. I rushed to the altar in my home in Houston, held on to the Master's Divine Padukas, and cried out. Literally within seconds, the very person who had hurled abuses on the phone just a minute ago, called me back, apologized and built the bridge back. Do I call this a miracle? Yes, it was, but it never registered that way. Till date, I carry in my heart that it was the Master's compassion that made the 180 degree turn of events, when the odds of that was impossible.

If it was a miracle, I'd have to first assume a state of 'normalcy' that the Master was in, that he'd then have to step up to execute the miracle, and then go back again to a steady state. What we have here is not that at all. The Master is ever compassionate. When the prayer reaches him, we connect to the grace. We feel it.

~~

A few episodes over the course of time continue to reveal how the Guru's grace is ever present. Many of these are silly events that could be dismissed by our minds on a routine day, but when open to the acceptance that grace is running our lives, the whole life becomes a treasure to keep.

We were once hosting a Bhagavata Saptaha Utsav celebration event in Houston. The celebration was for 7 days, but the planning and preparation consumed us for well over two months.

It was the onset of winter, and the grass had stopped growing. We usually hire a gardener who takes care of the yard at home once every couple of weeks, but with the weather being cold, we had asked him to come only on request and not regularly as in the other seasons. It had been more than 2 months since anyone took care of the yard. Just like how when a *sadhak*[62] stops his spiritual practice somehow the mind gets automatically occupied by unnecessary thoughts, the grass had stopped growing, and weeds had taken over. The backyard was a mess.

We hadn't stepped out or looked at the yard in a long time, given that we were so tied up with the events and were barely home. When the event was wrapped up and we came back home and sat down, that's when I noticed the yard through the window. I walked out and was shocked to see the dilapidated state in which the once-beautiful garden was.

Geez, how poorly we have cared for the yard all this time, I thought. I'll admit that the thought crossed my mind that it was the satsang that took away my focus. In a moment though, I repented whole-heartedly for thinking thus, and rushed back into the house. It was freezing outside.

The moment I came back in the house, someone rang the front door bell. It was unusual, as we weren't expecting anyone at that time. When I opened the door, my

---

[62] serious spiritual aspirant

good old gardener was there smiling at me, asking if there was any job for him!

What to say of the Lord's grace? Now, is this some miracle? No. It's just a little experience the Lord gives to show that it was always He who takes care of everything. It was a reinforcement of the presence of grace.

~~

I used to listen to the Pancha Stuti[63] CD every morning. One of the prayers was Gajendra Stuti[64]. One day, as I was listening to it, this one phrase towards the end of the prayer just got stuck in my head - *'shakti trayAya akhiladIgunAya'*. I just couldn't get it out of my head. I kept saying this particular line over and over again. I didn't know what it meant except that it had something to do with three *shaktis* (powers), but for some strange and unknown reason it ate up all my thoughts.

I was washing the worship utensils that morning as I listened to the stutis. *'Shakti TrayAya'* kept running in my head as I was washing the *harathi*[65] plate. When I flipped the plate over, I observed the imprinted product name. The

---

[63] Five famous prayer hymns from Srimad Bhagavatam
[64] The beautiful prayer by Gajendra, the elephant. SB 8.3
[65] An elongated plate used in Hindu worship rituals

make was 'Shakti', and right below that word, the number 3 was circled. It shocked me totally as I stared at the metal plate that literally read *'shakti trayAya'* just as my tongue got frozen with those very same words in the stuti. I had washed that same plate a hundred times before and never noticed the markings behind it. I wrestled with my mind on what this could mean, until a wise man told me that this how is how we become aware of the presence of grace, which is there at all times, but we are often blind to its presence. When we are open to His grace, we become aware of its presence. We don't necessarily need great miracles or life changing events to perceive grace.

~~

Once a handful of satsang friends were having some fun, playing together. There was a 12-year-old there who happened to have an electronic game. It was a handheld toy called 20 Questions. This is how the game worked – the player should first think of something...anything. The artificial-intelligence-computer-programmed toy would then ask a series of 20 questions, for which the player should answer either Yes, No, Sometimes, or Unknown. The toy would then try to guess whatever the player was thinking of.

This toy is incredible. It guesses everything right. We tried many things with this, thinking of anything from iPod to Cereal bars. The toy was on its game that day. We collectively put our heads together and schemed to beat it. We thought of 'God'.

Its first question was: Is it smaller than a loaf of bread? We said yes. Is it heavier than an elephant? We said yes. We kept going. We answered all the 20 questions quite vaguely because we knew God would fit into all the definitions it was trying to corner us into. Was it a man? Yes. It lived in water? Yes. There was no way for this toy to know what we were thinking, for nothing (or everything!) in the world would fit the definition of God. We were so eagerly waiting for the end of the round to see what it would say. 20 questions later, it caved in. Its ego was partly beat. It sheepishly said it needed more time. It asked us to extend the game for 5 more questions. We didn't make a fuss. We said ok, you got it. We gave more vague answers. Was it an insect? Yes. Could it speak Spanish? Yes! We were laughing away as even a million questions would not be useful.

After 25 questions, it couldn't take it anymore. It gave out its pre-programmed drumroll, followed with the answer: "Him (As in me myself)"

We looked at each other in disbelief, yet unsure what it really meant. 'Him' could be God, and "As in me myself' could be the God within us. We knew this was some deep philosophical thing that had God written all over it.

How could this thing know? It was super human! It was rigged, we thought. Finally it was our egos that were crashed.

A few days later, one person from this group went to India, and had the Master's darshan. They gave him a book and asked for his blessings. The Master opened the book and wrote in the first page: "Krishna is within you and within me". That's when it hit us. When we play with God, He will play with us.

~~

When I went to India later in the year, I wanted to have the Master's beautiful blessing words on a book and presented my prayer. The Master wrote:

"It is possible for me to feel Krishna's grace is pouring on Sriram – G"

He gives, and he perceives it, I thought. Not stopping with that, he even writes it down and signs it, without having to make me go through sorrows to figure out the grace working. This is compassion.

A True Reflection

"Who says the Lord doesn't speak? The voice of the conscience is the voice of the Lord," says the Master in his divine work, *Kali Dharma Undiyaar*. This voice of the conscience is ever there, unlike even the voices of the nearest and dearest in the family or friends, which are fleeting in nature.

It tells us what is right from wrong. Now what we do with it, is a different question. Whether we abide, ignore, or rebel is our choice, but the voice is always there - independent, unaffected, and unbiased.

The Master says that the Guru is like a mirror. Why does everyone like the Guru?

People have differences of opinion and quarrels, even within satsangs. Just like how only dirty laundry comes to the cleaners, the Master says it is only those who need to be cleaned that come to a Guru. But who wants to admit their impurities to the Master? Don't we all want to put our best impressions in front of him?

But the beauty of the Master is that he always reflects only what we want him to acknowledge of us. If we want him to recognize us for something, he'll do just that. If we would rather sit in the back benches and quietly mind our business, he allows that and walks without saying a word. If we want him to joke with us, he'll be greatest source of joy one can imagine. If we want him to play with us, we better have a prayer, for we cannot compete with him.

The Master has written a kirtan on Krishna that goes *Sangaruchir Manava Sahaja SwabhAvaha.* The essence of the kirtan is, whatever company we seek in this world, we can get the highest representation of it in Krishna; so choose Him. If we like the company of the wealthy, seek the company of the Consort of Lakshmi, the goddess of wealth. If we like the company of a scholar, seek the Disciple of Sandeepani. If we like the company of a beautiful baby, seek the company of the Darling of Gokula. And so forth the kirtan goes.

The Master is no different, I'd say. With a professor, he can talk about their subject, *whatever* it may be; to a child, he goes down to his level; with a teenager, he can discuss the most contemporary gadgets; with a Vedic pandit, he can delve deep into the scriptures. The Master is a mirror. He reflects what we are and what we want him to say. Despite knowing our most intimate thoughts and capabilities, he will never ever make it known that he knows it. We feel absolutely comfortable in his presence; just as comfortable as each of us would be in a private room in front of a mirror.

During one of the annual Janmashtami Brahmotsav festivals in the Ashram, I got the great fortune of carrying one of the sides of the palanquin that carried the Divine Couple[66] during processions. The Master was at the head of the procession, and while being a palanquin-bearer is a great opportunity for service, selfishly speaking it is also a great vantage point from where the Master's darshan is never blocked. For several days I got this fortunate job. The 10-day festival ended joyously. A week later there was

---

[66] Sri Krishna-Sri Radha

another one-day event, Radhashtami - the birthday of Sri Radha Devi.

The crowd on this day was light, say a few hundred people only, not in the thousands as in the previous week. The Master had wished for a procession that day. We were all waiting and I was called by one of the organizers to lift one side of the palanquin. I went quite happily but did not get the front side, but only the rear. I didn't complain. I said to myself that this was a *kainkarya* (service) and no service is lesser than another. But secretly, I was a little disappointed as I wouldn't be able to see the Master at all from the back. Nevertheless, it was a blessing, I consoled myself.

The Master began with a few kirtans and I was trying to sneak a view here and there without dropping my end of the palanquin. It wasn't fun beyond the first 10 minutes. My single focus was on the hidden Master, but his was surely on the Lord, not to mention the hundreds of others in front of the procession. I was stuck in the back, invisible to him as well. Why would he think of my plight? I whined to myself.

At that moment, I was able to sense there was some conversation near the Master. He had whispered something to someone nearby. That man came to my side of the palanquin, and said to me, "Guruji has asked you to come in the front and sing." And he took over my duty. I was elated to say the least! On the pretext of making me come over to sing, he gave me his beautiful darshan, which is exactly what I wanted. The singing part was now a bonus too.

When a bhagavata completed a song he was singing, the Master looked in my direction and asked me to sing a *namavali*[67]. I sang an old, rarely sung Tamil bhajan '*Radhe Radhe Radhe*'. The Master was very pleased. In the middle of the kirtan, a line goes '*Radhe Radhe Radhe is our goal. We will attain this (enlightenment) with no other spiritual practice (but chanting Radhe Radhe Radhe!)*'. When I sang this line, the Master turned and looked at me in wonder, and admired that line so much. Everyone wondered what kirtan this was, as this was something they had never heard before.

Sri Poornimaji, during her US visits, had taught us this bhajan, which was written a few years ago by the Master himself. Many devotees in the US know this kirtan,

---

[67] A short, lilting song that consists primarily of the Names of God

but none in India knew it. Even the Master did not remember that it was his own kirtan!

Poornimaji who was also there at the procession that day, told a few people nearby that this was indeed the Master's song. The kirtan ended with a reverberating chant of "Radhe Radhe" for a few minutes. When it ended, the Master turned in my direction and asked, "What kirtan is this? Whose is this?"

I said smilingly, "This is Guruji's kirtan only." His reaction to that was the most priceless. He grinned from ear to ear, with surprise and admiration.

The Master often quotes a story of how Krishna once went to Radha's house and climbed up a flight of stairs to go up to Radha's room. At the turn of the stairs, there was a full-sized mirror. When the innocent Krishna saw Himself in the mirror, He was so surprised and elated about how beautiful the person in the mirror looked. He called out, "Radhe, come and see this! Who is this beautiful youth? I have never seen anyone so good looking!" Radha came out, wondering what Krishna was talking about, for in her mind, there was no one else of that description but Krishna himself. When she saw who Krishna was looking at, she laughed and said, "That is you, Krishna! It's a mirror! It's your own reflection in the mirror. You are the one who is so beautiful."

When I saw the Master's reaction when he realized that that beautiful kirtan was his own, I thought this is exactly how Krishna must have reacted to Radha – with that unforgettable look with a tinge of surprise, admiration, innocence, shyness, laughter – all rolled into one unique and most beautiful darshan I've ever had.

Nothing mundane about it

The Master often quotes the story of a devotee of
Sri Ramakrishna Paramahamsa – Girish Chandra Ghosh – to
highlight the greatness of a Guru. For us, even the stories of
the greatest devotees of the Lord like Prahlada and Narada
may not be inspiring enough, but the lives of devotees like
Ajamila[68] and Girish Chandra Ghosh gives us the much
needed confidence that we too can succeed in this journey
of life. Ajamila and Girish were caught up in the clutches of
the greatest vices known to mankind. In the case of Girish,
it was the sheer grace of his Guru, Sri Ramakrishna, that
made Girish see his Master in everything from wine and
women to everything in between, thus reforming him
completely.

---

[68]A fallen man who led a degraded, sinful life but was redeemed in his last breath
because he providentially called out to the Lord (actually called out to his son who
happened to be named after the Lord). SB 6:1-3

How the Guru works on us is a thing of beauty. In just a simple enquiry they can change our whole life. Well, why go that far as an enquiry; even a split second thought about us is sufficient. Yet, out of their unbounded compassion, they choose to engage with us, and talk to us - sometimes seriously, and at other times, appearing quite mundane. But nothing from their perspective is mundane, for they take even the most mundane looking conversation into something absolutely divine.

The Master always says that no one is ever bored of three things in this world. The full moon, the ocean, and the elephant. We could just stare at the full moon all night, or just be at the beach and stare at the ocean endlessly, and never get bored. The elephant too is always a great attraction to everyone from the tiny toddler to the great-grandpa in the house. When talking about the full moon, the Master casually comments – *"Isn't this the same moon that Lord Rama and Lord Krishna saw when they came down to the earth as incarnations?"* That comment was all that it took for me. I could never look at the moon again without connecting to this quote. A view of the moon always reminds me of the Master and his deep and thoughtful connection to divinity. Same with the ocean and the elephant, and many other mundane things that are now automatically divine because it connects me back to the Master.

Once the Master was in one such mood where he was connecting everything to the Lord. He said, "See this woodpecker – how unique is this creature! It pecks only four times, takes a break and then four more. It's not random. There is a definite pattern. How wonderful is this Lord's creation!" Then the Master went on and on about so many different animals and their uniqueness. From then on, I cannot help but naturally think about the Master when I encounter such beings.

In another conversation, he talked to me about how politicians live very long lives. He would have quoted at least a half a dozen names in quick succession who are into their 80's and 90's and still active, to show that activity and passionate work is key. I left with a new found admiration for work.

The Master may touch casually on any seemingly mundane or worldly subject – slavery, musicians, autism, trees, animals, trains, vacations, entertainment or anything else. However, slowly but surely, the impact of these conversations with the Master, have made such powerful imprint that even these seemingly worldly mentions have a deeper purpose.

Whether the world teaches me a moral is a different story, the fact that the world reminds me of the Lord is the point.

Mahamantra, as I see it

Hare Rama Hare Rama Rama Rama Hare Hare |
Hare Krishna Hare Krishna Krishna Krishna Hare Hare ||

The heart and soul of the Master is the Mahamantra. To take this Divine Name to every nook and corner of the world is the purpose of this incarnation of the divine.

Why the Divine Name? Why this mantra specifically? Should it be Hare Rama first or Hare Krishna first? Does chanting this once make a difference? If so, why is there a need to chant always? What's the significance of initiation? Is a Guru needed to chant this? How come there are no rules? How can a small mantra with no rules be so potent?

For the record, I had none of these questions.

A group of middle-school aged youth were once very eager to ask a lot of questions about our culture and religion to a visiting sadhu. Among them was one particularly curious boy. He would raise his hand and ask a question. When it was answered, instantly he would raise his hand again with another question, and then another one, and another, and so it went. The expert patiently answered the first few, then gave the other children a chance. The boy raised his hand once again. The speaker quickly put him in his place saying, "You're interested in only asking questions. Not finding the answers."

It was a lesson for me too. I used to have a lot of questions initially, but over time learned that clarity truly dawns, not when questions are answered, but when questions go away.

All of those important questions about the Mahamantra have perfectly valid answers but it's not my intent to write about that here. Any lecture by the Master on the Mahamantra will explain it far more lucidly than I can put in words.

My journey in this *"raja margam"*[69] (royal path) started in 2007 with the birth of my daughter. From that very day, the seed of Mahamantra within me had also started to grow. The first chants were merely a stress reliever, and a prayer when my daughter came into this world. I was able to hold onto something while a major life event was underway. Without that hold, the mind would have gone nuts.

Even back then, the routine monthly one-hour chanting on the 21st of each month was not something I looked forward to. It started out with respect for the request from my mother-in-law, and then gradually became a mechanical chore. But there is no doubt that it was that chanting that led us to the ocean of the Sadguru's grace!

When I visited India in late 2007, I had another moment-of-truth-test experience. My father underwent an open-heart valve replacement surgery. This happened on a Wednesday. I was scheduled to leave back to the US three days later, on Saturday. The surgery was successfully completed on Wednesday evening. But no visitors were

---

[69] The famous saint Sri Thyagaraja sings in one of his songs – *Chakkani raja margamu* – "When there is the royal path to reach you, O Rama (simply chanting Rama's Name), why resort to bylanes (more difficult paths)?"

allowed for 24 hours. On the other hand, all through the three-week trip, I had been pondering about requesting formal initiation from the Master. My trip was down to the last two days and I still had not done anything about it.

On Thursday morning, I had the most serious urge to have the darshan of the Master. Never before had I felt this kind of an intensity.

But it was also the most pivotal day in the life of my father, who was coming out of a major surgery and it would be sacrilege to even suggest skipping the hospital visit to go have the Master's darshan. Even the Master would not like this idea. An especially important point to note is that I was the only one in my family who had any interest with the Master and his satsang. So there was really no room for discussion.

To make matters worse, I learned that the Master was leaving for a trip down to south Tamil Nadu on Friday morning. So I had absolutely no option. I had to either meet the Master that day, or not have the darshan till my next visit to India, which would be a year or two away. Unlike the cricket match test in the previous month, this one was more serious on many fronts.

I couldn't visit the hospital in the morning because visiting hours were only after 6 PM. If I waited that long and then started on my long journey to the Ashram, I couldn't make it there any earlier than 8 PM, which would be too late. It came down to whether I should skip the Master's darshan and spend time at the hospital, or vice-versa. As before, by God's grace, my frame of mind left me with no choice – I had to have the Master's darshan. It was the most important thing.

Close to sunset, I booked a long distance cab to the ashram, but en route, I stopped at the hospital to see my father in the ICU. All was well.

I raced out of the hospital and was on the way to the Ashram. Ten minutes into the drive, I received a call from the Master's personal secretary. He said, "Guruji has changed his plan. He will come to Chennai in the morning. You can turn around and go now. Come tomorrow at 9 AM to Premika Bhavanam."

This is how the Master works. This is how compassion works. I was one among a million. He is the Almighty. I needed to do what I did. He need not have done what he did, I thought. But the only way the Lord could have balanced my needs was to do what he did. He changed his plans to make mine easier. Who would do that?

I went back and spent time with my family and didn't face any backlash for the decision I had made earlier. The next morning, I went to Premika Bhavanam and amidst Bhagavata *parayana*[70], the Master bestowed His grace and initiation on me right in the middle of the hall. Overcome with gratitude, I prostrated again and again to the compassion incarnate.

I informed him that my father had had an open heart surgery the previous day, and prayed for his speedy recovery. The compassionate Master took a fruit, kept it close to his heart and prayed silently. He then gave me the fruit and signed that all will be well. Needless to say, my dad had the fastest ever recovery back to normalcy. Within a couple of months, the ever-energetic person that he is, was back on his two-wheeler weaving in and out of the busy roads of Chennai. Things were indeed normal!

~~

The initiation from the Guru is not procedural or trivial. It makes a change at a level imperceptible to the

---

[70] Recitation/reading of the original Srimad Bhagavatam Sanskrit text

senses. How we perceive this change is only by a look back at how our lives have changed since that day.

~~

My parents were not as focused as me on the Master. But individuals even within the same household do connect to him at varied paces, though from his side, the connection had already been established. A few years ago, my family went out to a theme park in California with my visiting parents. It was a beautiful summer day and we were hopping away through all the kiddie rides with our 6-year-old and some of her cousins. We came upon this seemingly innocent rollercoaster and my daughter convinced my mother to get on the ride. My mother wasn't comfortable at all but with the loving request of her granddaughter she obliged reluctantly. She looked at the previous riders carefully to prepare herself mentally for the not-so-joyful-ride. You could see her sweat. She just wasn't comfortable but before she could back out, the helpers there secured her into the seat, put the belt on, and the whistle blew.

My wife and I were sitting in the front. Suddenly, I heard loud chanting: Hare Rama Hare Rama Rama Rama Hare Hare; Hare Krishna Hare Krishna Krishna Krishna Hare

Hare! The faster the rollercoaster moved, the faster went the chanting. I was super thrilled. And the thrill of the rollercoaster was dull in comparison.

My mother was chanting Nama when fear gripped her! Before this incident, I felt she hadn't taken to Nama, but only now could I see the impact it had on her. She knew many other slokas but it was the Mahamantra that she chanted when divine help was needed. The Mahamantra had gone into her subconsciously and started to work the magic.

~~

Whether we like it or not, when Nama is in the household, it attacks everyone like a benign virus. The Master likens Nama to termites. Each termite may seem small and insignificant, but collectively it can bring down a house. It has that power. Likewise, as more and more Nama is chanted, it can destroy sins and ego, one after another, and finally Nama itself can lead us to permanent happiness.

We can talk at length about how prayers with the Divine Names are very powerful, by quoting scriptures and lives of saints, but nothing gives confidence like having a lifesaving experience ourselves.

It was the wedding anniversary of my parents a few years ago. We went out boating with a couple of satsang families on a large lake near Houston, to celebrate. We were 11 people in total and had a whale of a time on our self-driven rented boat for the first hour or so. It was a breezy evening, and it had started to make the lake a bit choppy. We had just cut the cake, played in the water on the shore of an island, and had had loads of fun. We got back on the boat and started our ride back to the dock area to return the boat. About a half a mile or so away, my friend and I noticed a strange-looking wave coming across the lake from left to right. We were a safe distance away and never really felt threatened. As it was getting dark, we decided to beat the funny wave by racing the boat faster in the hope of navigating around it before it hit us. But as destiny would have it, it moved closer and closer to our boat and we were trapped. We were bang in the middle of the lake, which was a hundred plus feet deep at that point and this large wave slammed on our boat. Water started to collect inside the boat and the front end of the flat pontoon boat started to taper down. We instructed everyone to move up to the top end of the boat. Some of our belongings - shoes, etc. - were washed away. Death stared all 11 of us – from six years to seventy-six years old – in the face. Two full satsang families had a real possibility of getting wiped out.

Just then, like how Draupadi[71] cried out, "Govinda", the oldest lady in the boat screamed, "Hare Rama Hare Rama Rama Rama Hare Hare, Hare Krishna Hare Krishna Krishna Krishna Hare Hare!" We all joined, holding hands together and praying with the Mahamantra. Within seconds, a blue boat showed up out of nowhere, threw a rope onto ours and lifted up the sinking side of the boat. In a minute, calm was restored and lives were saved. We could barely thank the man. He reassured us and disappeared as swiftly as he had arrived to save us. We quietly drifted away from the scene, looking at each other in disbelief, on how the Lord in the form of the man in the blue boat saved us.

By now it was quite clear that, by the Guru's grace, the Mahamantra was clearly our lifeline. I wondered if it was the Guru's grace or the power of the Divine Name that works all this magic. When we praise the Guru for

---

[71] A queen who was dragged disgracefully into the court, and in the presence of great elders and kings, an attempt was made to disrobe her. When no one came to her rescue, she cried out helplessly to Lord Krishna – Govinda – and even though He was not physically present there, she was miraculously saved!

everything, he will dismiss the praise and credit Nama instead: "It's all happening due to the greatness of Nama." But don't we know that we cannot get this Nama in our lips at the right time, if not for the Guru's grace?

~~

When the Master gave the title to this book, 'Mahamantra As I See It', it raised some fundamental questions in me.

This is the sign of a great leader. All that is needed is a small prod from him, and it opens up our eyes to unseen realizations.

So why do I chant it? I asked myself. Is it a *sadhana* (spiritual practice)? Is it the *saadhya* (end result/fruit of spiritual practice)? Is it a means of prayer? Is it a communication mode with the divine? Is it to show gratitude to the Guru? Is it to stay true to the Guru's instructions? Is it to propagate the Master's vision? What else am I not thinking?

As a sadhana, this is very hard. To me, just sitting and chanting for a few minutes with undivided attention is a pipedream. If this is a spiritual practice, I haven't started yet. The Master says that people dismiss this easy path because, in their minds, they think that something as easy as chanting the Mahamantra cannot really bestow the greatest. After all, aren't we all coached all through our lives that one has to strive hard to achieve greatness?

The path of Nama is the simplest and the easiest, no doubt. But this is primarily about the rules (lack of) and eligibility. That's where Nama is simple. The whole idea about Nama being dismissible as a spiritual path simply because it is easy, didn't add up to me. Because chanting Nama may appear easy but it is not. Let people try and chant for 20 minutes without fidgeting around, and then try that for an hour, and then six hours and upwards. It's a myth to think this is an easy path, in that sense. The ways of Maya (the Lord's deluding power) are indeed subtle.

If Nama is the saadhya, the very fact that I clearly know that I'm riddled with faults, makes me feel completely ineligible to be the recipient of this award. Great saints have vouched that the Divine Names cannot be uttered by our tongues unless we have acquired many merits in the past. I don't deny this is truth, but I'm just not able to feel it now. Nama as a saadhya is quite theoretical to me, just as much as 'unconditional love' and 'constant state of gratitude', because I'm not there yet.

I once prayed to the Master to give me the taste to chant the Names. "I understand that this is the path, but," I begged, "to proceed in it would be so much nicer if I was blessed with the taste for the Name. Right now, it's so mechanical."

The Master, in his own sweet way, said, "This is something the Lord will bestow by Himself at the right time."

I figured chanting is the practice, and getting the sweet taste of the Name is the real fruit.

And then there was – Nama as a prayer. Initially I never understood this purpose of Nama. Nor did I understand what true prayer was.

I once had the great fortune of traveling with a group of devotees of the Master to a series of mass prayers by the Master in deep interior Tamil Nadu. In one of the discourses – in Tuticorin – the Master spoke beautifully on how, as people, we have forgotten how to do bhakti and how to pray to God. He said, "Just communicating to God as if passing on a message, is not prayer. Prayer must be intense, deep, and a cry out to God."

The Master compares true prayer to how a newborn baby would cry out to the mother. All that it is going to say is "Ma!" and the mother knows if the child needs food, if it needs to be cleaned up, or just needs her affection. Likewise, all we need to do is cry out "Rama", "Krishna" and the Lord would know what we need.

As new devotees, we learn the ropes of how to place a prayer to the Master. We are advised to lay out the situation before him, explain all the known facts and leave any decisions to him completely. The most important warning here is that it is never a good idea to have a prayer with a result already in mind and seek blessings for that, because we never know what is truly best for us. After all, we have ourselves prayed for many things in life and wanted to reverse the course later. So leaving the choice entirely to the Master is the ideal prayer.

In that discourse in Tuticorin, the Master said, "Namadwaar is a school where we teach how to pray, and that prayer is by loudly crying out the Divine Names of the

Lord." By chanting aloud, we are crying out to God, we are explaining our situation. Chanting is surrender.

Draupadi didn't have to write a letter explaining all the facts about what was happening in the court, when she was being humiliated. Didn't the Lord protect her in an instant, when she gave it all up and shouted "Govinda"? It is that cry that is needed in prayer. It is the intensity.

When I'm in dire need of prayer, I need the method to be something that I can catch on immediately with my mind, with my tongue, with my actions, and orient it all together. I shouldn't have to worry about the rules, nor my state – whether I'm clean, facing the east, or sitting at the altar; nor whether I'm in India or elsewhere; or if it is the right time, right day, etc. When I have an intense prayer, I shouldn't have to recall complicated slokas, elaborate hymns or songs, seek a priest, go to a temple or even light a lamp or incense. Nothing. I shouldn't have to do any of this... because when I really need a prayer, I may not be in a position to do any of this. Yet I need a way to pray where I can rest assured that the means of prayer has the same potency in any situation; no less.

A chant is needed here too, with the prayer. Because without it, if the prayer was only a mental relay of my desire to God, even with a sincere intent, the human mind does not have the power to remain steadfast. Its nature is to waver, and with that vacillation, the connection to the divine also loses grip. The chanting helps to maintain the relationship with the divine and sustains the intensity of the prayer.

~~

"Maya" is a real threat for the seeker. This is more tangible and closer than the Lord himself, for I already experience it. The Master jovially says that the three incarnations of Maya these days are TV, cellphone, and the Internet. I remember this quote is dated back to the early millennium. Had it been 2015, I guess it wouldn't have to use three incarnations. We have beautifully organized all three avatars of Maya into one fascinating device – 'the *phablet'* – that has truly touched everyone in the world. What the Master had said jokingly was not a joke, after all.

The Master says that Maya's methods need not only be as concrete and tangible as an electronic distraction; it often plays a mean game simply using our minds. Just when we sit down to chant, the Master says there are two 'demons' it sends – the *karna pishachas* (ear ghosts)! They come and sit on our ears and begin their advice. One constantly says, "You've done enough chanting already. Why not do it later?" The other is less kind. It says, "What a waste of time! Don't ever do this!" When these two demons sit on either ears, it will surely take a miracle for a seeker of happiness to make progress.

The Master also says that Maya takes an even subtler form, when it uses 'freedom' – the very opposite of slavery – to bind us. The Master defines Maya as that which makes us unsure whether there is freewill or not. That doubt that we all have is Maya. The perception of total freedom is the trap. Oh how subtle and devious this thing is. It is cruel.

The more 'learned' we become in this world, the subtler and stronger the trap gets. Sometimes, I feel I just want to be a simpleton with blind faith. It would make life so much easier. But alas! That ship has long sailed; and now unwinding from this mess seems the only way out.

Thankfully, we have the perfect path – one that satisfies the mind as well as the intellect, while going easy on the qualification. There seems to be no other way.

When it needs to be, the Divine Name can be a hard pill and impossible to swallow. Let's try chanting loudly with closed eyes for one hour. When Maya plays hardball with tangible distractions, we now have a hard means out of it.

The subtler the distraction, the subtler Nama can get. Like when the ear demons attack us, just murmuring the Divine Names on the lips, even mechanically, would suffice. It keeps them away.

When the distraction is even subtler, like the never-ending mental tussle of freewill vs. destiny, just mentally chanting the Divine Name in an even subtler manner would never even bring forth such a confusion. For even the question will not arise when the counter attack of the Divine Name operates at the thought (mind) level.

While the chant itself is supremely potent and I have no doubt about that, it is the universality that appealed most to me. There is nothing else in the world that applies so universally to everything and everyone, regardless of any bias or requirements. This is the only thing in the world that is capable of bringing us all together in peace, be it for personal prayers, for uniting families, uniting people across borders, faiths, and races, and at the same time tackling Maya – the greatest personal hurdle imposed by the Lord Himself.

This is how I see the Mahamantra.

With all due respect to the million ways and faiths through which one may seek God and Happiness, I have not heard of one that is bereft of any rules. Even within Sanatana Dharma (Hinduism) there is so much variety in worship. But chanting the Divine Names is the only one that I feel I'm eligible for. It is not only that there are no rules, but also the fact that it is the only thing that can be done at every moment, at every place. It's the only thing that can permeate through space and time – I can chant it in my bathroom or in a library, with or without others, in my mind or loudly, with no difference in the outcome. What other way of prayer can offer this breadth of application?

The more I think of Nama, not only do I get convinced, but I also feel there is no other way.

~~

Once I had the fortune of staying in the ashram for a day while the Master was also there. Very early in the morning, I went to Bhagavata Bhavanam, the large hall which is the *darbar* (court) of the Master's deities Sri Madhuri Sakhi and Sri Premika Varadan (Sri Radha and Sri Krishna). I was chanting the Mahamantra along with a couple of ashram residents. The Master walked up to my side and asked, "Will you sing *prabodhanam*[72] today?"

While I was elated that the Master spoke a word to me, I was utterly nervous because I didn't know any of those songs, nor could I just make up the tunes. I nervously nodded my head in affirmation. How could I say no!

"Now, you are the *Asthana vidwan*[73]!" the Master joked and laughed as he walked by. Usually during satsangs and celebrations, the ashram is filled with great singers. But today since the ashram is literally empty, he is stuck with me, I thought.

The Master went inside the altar while the screen was still closed, I hurriedly opened the kirtan book and was wondering where to start. Suddenly the Master's voice

---

[72] A way of waking up the Lord with kirtan
[73] The prime or resident musician of a court of kingdom

came from inside, "Sriram, hmm… begin." The song in Bhoopala raga was somewhat straight forward and I managed to sing that. Then came all the unfamiliar songs in variety of ragas – Bilahari, Mohanam, Behag and what not. I had no idea about the songs, nor the tunes, or the words. I hastily signed for an ashram resident nearby to help me. She came and sang the rest of the songs, while I played second fiddle. Clearly the Master must have enjoyed this, and Premika Varadan too could not have had a ruder awakening!

Somehow the prabodhanam adventure was completed. The Master walked out of the altar and signed for a devotee to repeat the Mahamantra after him. He then asked a couple of ladies to sit on the other side and alternate the chanting. I stood leaning against a wall. The Master turned towards me and signed for me to join as well. I was thrilled by the inclusion into this small group of chanters with the Master. I went and stood behind one of the devotees. The Master sat down and continued to chant. Everyone else did the same. At that time, the Master turned and looked at me, tapped his palm on the floor next to him and nodded, asking me to come and sit next to him. I went and sat down, and continued to chant. I could tell that the Master was really enjoying this chanting. In a minute, he tapped on my left thigh and said, "Close your eyes and chant. Don't open till instructed."

I shut my eyes that second and the only thing I could perceive from that point forward was the voice of the Master, alternating with mine. In Sindhubhairavi raga, the Master chanted, "Hare Rama Hare Rama Rama Rama Hare Hare, Hare Krishna Hare Krishna Krishna Krishna Hare Hare."

With the divine presence around me, I could smell the divinity in the ambience. My ears were glued to the Master's voice; my eyes imagined his presence right next to me. I relived again and again his split second pat. And for the first time, I could taste the sweetness of the chanting. Above all, my mind, which always races away in a million different directions the moment I sit down to chant, was calm and quiet.

I know the status of my mind. It wavers and oscillates, looks for excuses to stop chanting, and eagerly seeks out distractions. Every ding on the phone is always the perfect excuse to stray. But in those minutes with the

Master by my side, I knew my mind went nowhere but focused exclusively on his voice, trying to catch it like a lifeline. It was 'in the moment' and one-pointed.

Suddenly the Master's deep voice resonated with a heartfelt prayer[74], "Krishna, give me unwavering devotion to Your feet (pause); give me wisdom and dispassion." We repeated. The Master repeated this prayer a few times.

After some more chanting, the Master continued the prayer[75], "May Your Divine Name be always on my tongue." We repeated. The Master continued to say these two prayers a few times, and then proceeded with chanting the Mahamantra.

The pleasant chanting and prayer experience with the Master continued like an undisturbed flow of oil for the next 30 minutes or so. I was absolutely enjoying the chanting.

But then, in a flash, the Master's voice stopped; and so did my heart. I didn't know what to do. The rest of the voices continued to chant. Since my instruction was to keep my eyes closed, I couldn't just open my eyes and see what

---

[74] Original prayer in Tamil: *Krishna, un charaNatthile asanchalamAna bhaktiyai kuDu; jnAna vairAgyatthai kuDu.*
[75] In Tamil: *eppozhudhum ennuDaya nAvil un nAmam thavazhndhu konDe irukkaTTum.*

was going on. For a minute, all my senses appeared to lock up, and the only feeling I was left with was fear. Like I was left all alone in a forest with no one around. I stopped chanting, unable to comprehend my next step. For the first time ever, I truly missed the Master. His absence took me to a state of fear, not knowing where I was headed and how I was going to get out of this blindness. He didn't give me any further instruction, nor was he there physically, with his comforting voice, touch or smell. Sri Ramuji, who was chanting right next to me, realized my state of silence, and tapped on my other thigh and asked me to continue chanting.

I gathered myself together and continued. A few minutes later, I was 'instructed' to take a break for breakfast. That was when I opened my eyes. It had been an hour and I hadn't realized that at all. It had gone quite briskly. After breakfast, I came back and sat in the same place, promptly closed my eyes and continued to chant, trying to get back the 'experience'. The second round of chanting lasted another couple of hours, though the experience was no longer there. I searched eagerly for it, but I could never fully get to the same calmness there was when the Master was next to me. My mind went back to its wandering nature, while the tongue continued to chant.

That's when it hit me like a lightning on what the Master's presence meant. When the Guru wills, even the most insurmountable obstacle (the mind) can be overcome effortlessly. In fact, only by his grace can that happen. No amount of self-effort can bring that happiness, but a mere graceful glance of the Guru can quieten the mind.

When the Master made me close my eyes and chant, I could see – through the Guru's grace – how the Mahamantra worked. When the Master named this book, 'Mahamantra As I See It', I didn't quite understand the depth of it. Maybe I'll never fathom the grandness of all the words that come out of him. Through this experience, the Master taught me that it's not the physical eyes that are needed to see, but the mind's eyes. And it is that eye that the Master wishes to open by his grace, by closing the attractions of the world from the physical eyes.

And all this for what? Absolutely nothing! The Master's grace has no reason. It's always there. Just showing up, and being a vessel, is all that is needed from our side.

The Revolution

With great fortune, I have reached your feet
I prostrate again and again to You, O Guru!

I roamed about the world with not a care
You took over my life with Your unbounded grace

Being one above and beyond name and form,
To establish the Divine Names in the world,
You came down with a name and a form
And go about the world singing the Lord's Names!

The above lines are a translation of the Master's Tamil song *Bhagyavasathal Un Tiruvadi Adaindhen* on the greatness of the Guru. For us it applies perfectly to the relationship we have with the Master.

I was roaming about the world with no sense of purpose, vision, gratitude, or love. I didn't know why, but somehow due to the Master's endless mercy, he made me too, a recipient of that grace.

Be it a saint, an aspirant, a nobleman, a good citizen, a ruffian, or be it someone like me – the definition of an average fellow – the Master's vision will gracefully fall on every person in the world.

~~

The Master looks at this world and relishes the beauty in it. He always implores us to notice how beautifully the peacock dances, how sweet the cuckoo sings. "Do you see the beauty in a butterfly's wings? Who made it thus? Have you seen the ants' colonies? Who taught it to build such a complex yet masterful construction that puts modern day engineers to shame?"

We are talking ants! How grand is this universe. How perfectly the planets and the moon position themselves day in and day out. How promptly the sun rises and sets at prescribed times. How does the ocean set a boundary and not cross it? How is it possible that the five elements – the earth, water, fire, air, and space – each naturally antagonistic to one another, coexist in perfect unison in this world?

There is order in everything, and such order just doesn't happen by chance. It is God who has set everything up so that one day we delve into the bigger questions of life and seek Him. Being so compassionate, He has given us this world to enjoy in until we get to the point of seeking Him. That's when the Guru enters.

When the Lord who created this magnificent universe is also the Lord of Maya, is it any surprise that the whole population is completely enamored by it? Now, if the Lord can make Maya so powerful, how much more powerful would He make Himself when He comes down to take us ashore?

This power that the Master has come with is the power of Love, with his biggest weapon – the Divine Name. The revolution has begun. The whole world will chant the Mahamantra very soon. This is the vision of the Lord, and the Master is here to show us the way. With that vision, the Master has already established 20 Namadwaar Prayer Houses – many in India and several worldwide too, including Sydney-Australia, Singapore, Kuala Lumpur-Malaysia, and Houston-USA.

A couple of years ago, when I visited the ashram, I was chanting and praying in the main hall one early afternoon. Suddenly a *Veda patashala*[76] student tapped on my shoulder and asked if I was Sriram. I nodded, "Yes." He said, "Guruji is calling you." Oh how can one explain the joy that is felt when the Master calls? I ran in to the Master's room.

The mood was intense, the ambience very quiet. The Master was seated on his chair. I went and stood by his side awaiting the great blessing that was going to come out of the divinity that day. He got up from his chair and walked back and forth, deep in thought.

With a deep breath, he leaned on the wall. He tilted his head upwards and called out in anguish, "Premika Varadaa...!" After a long pause, he turned and looked in my direction, "Nama should spread all over America." He then named half-a-dozen cities and said, "Many Namadwaars should come up all over America. This should happen in our

---

[76] A school for the study of the Vedas – the primary Hindu scripture. The Master's Madhurapuri Ashram houses a Veda patashala.

life time itself. We should experience this ourselves, and not only the future generations. We should work very hard for this. Go and pray to Premika Varadan for this to happen successfully!"

It is the Master's wish that the whole world will have many more such spiritual centers that will show the current and future generations how to pray and find a lifeline in these times.

There's no magic, no miracles, no false promises, no money involved, no name, no fame, no self-interest. Only God.

The revolution in three grand steps:

Universal Harmony through Spiritual Awakening

Spiritual Awakening through Inner Transformation

Inner Transformation by Chanting the Divine Names

It's not a question of 'if' we want to be in this movement; rather, I believe, it is a question of 'when'! For in the present times, the Mahamantra shall always triumph – as it did with me.

Glories to the benign great mantra of love and divinity!

About the Author

Sriram lives in Houston, Texas, USA with his wife and daughter. By divine grace, Sriram came into his Master, His Holiness Maharanyam Sri Sri Muralidhara Swamiji's fold in 2007. Since then, he has been an active member of Global Organization for Divinity (G.O.D.) satsangs and Love to Share Foundation America's initiatives in the USA.

Since Namadwaar Prayer House was established by G.O.D. USA in Houston in February 2010, Sriram and his family have been blessed with numerous opportunities to serve their Master.

Sriram is an Industrial Engineer by qualification and works as a Supply Chain Manager for a Fortune 50 company in Houston.